Lady Up America

Training Christian Moms for the Toughest Spiritual Battleground of our Lifetime

Diane Canada

Nashville, Tennessee

Lady Up America

Training Christian Moms for The Toughest Spiritual Battleground of our Lifetime

"I am the vine; you are the branches. He who abides in Me, and I in him, bears much fruit; for without Me you can do nothing."

-John 15:5 (NKJV)

Table of Contents

Chapter One

We've Lost the Luxury of a Meltdown

I braced myself as I logged into Facebook to share another post from the campaign trail because I knew there would be mean-spirited comments waiting. Yes, that comes with the territory, and I probably shouldn't have read them, but I couldn't seem to help it. Running for State House of Representatives in 2020 would prove to be one of the most challenging things I would ever do.

Between covid mandates that polarized us, the lockdowns that were costing people their homes and businesses, the burning cities from BLM riots, and one of the most tumultuous Presidential elections of our lifetime, emotions were at an all-time high, to say the least. Social media was where everybody was taking out their frustrations. Comments from friends and strangers alike were vicious. I was devastated as lifelong friends I dearly loved walked away simply because they "couldn't believe I was a Republican".

And then, the unthinkable happened...

My adult son started joining in the chorus of public comments on Facebook. I went from being shocked that we didn't share the same values, to feeling hurt by his public show of disrespect, to being furious with him because of the destructive impact his behavior could have on my campaign.

I don't ever remember a time in his life that I have EVER been angry at my son, much less THAT angry. I didn't know how to handle it, so I gave in to my emotions. I indulged in a meltdown.

I reprimanded him in a furious voicemail, demanding that even if he had different views, we should talk about them privately out of respect for the fact that I'm still his mom. I'll admit heavy cursing occurred, as well. I'm not proud of that, just honest. I forgot he was an adult, talked to him like a child, and he responded in a way that I would have never wanted. He decided to stop communication between us.

The distance has been incredibly hard. I love him with every fiber of my being, and I've cried a river of tears. He and I have both apologized to each other and we're slowly trying to find our way back, but it will take time. The differences in our ideologies are still there, but when I indulged in my meltdown, I lost all credibility, access, and ability to influence him. I mean I really blew it, and the emotional cost has been significant.

So many of my girlfriends have gone through the exact same struggle with their adult children. They live with the same pain, and we have comforted and prayed over each other countless times. This epidemic of political division within families, and our inability to handle it, is destroying families. I went into the deepest depths of prayer, begging God for healing, not just for me and my son, but for all the other families that were going through the same pain. That's when the breakthrough happened.

I had a divine "ah-ha moment" in 2021!

Since that moment, God has been revealing things to me, slowly and profoundly, in what I call **the best "drip campaign", ever**! It has led to the development of Lady Up America. Let me share the quick version of this journey to my divine ah-ha moment.

I never wanted to run for Office. Politics was never on my radar. It was something God called me to do after the loss of my brother, a Special Ops Marine who served in Afghanistan and came home with a brain injury and severe PTSD. We lost him one week before Christmas in 2015. That is a call I wouldn't wish on any family. I can still feel the ache in my stomach.

I ran for Office to address the practical struggles our veterans face when trying to re-enter civilian life, to offer creative solutions, and to try and prevent other families from experiencing what we went through. The only problem is that you don't get to just focus on one thing when you run for Office. You're required to go on the record about your position on a variety of topics that I had never stopped to consider before.

I was pretty sure I was a Republican, but I didn't know WHY.

- How *did* I feel about abortion?

- What *was* my stand on the 2nd Amendment?

- *Did* BLM have a valid point?

These are things I was now required to address…and FAST! So, I began to study like a beast! I started down a path of exploration into all these topics and SO many more! I didn't want to stay in an echo chamber, so I took people to lunch who held opposing views to my Party and tried to understand both sides. I spent time in lower-income neighborhoods and schools trying to get a better understanding of their day-to-day struggles.

I spent a LOT of time getting to know my Legislators. I spent entire days in the Tennessee Capitol, sitting in on hearings, and shadowing leaders for the day. I took courses in the Constitution, history courses, and was accepted into a Political Leadership course to learn as much context as possible. I wanted to understand the issues thoroughly, develop my platform responsibly, and represent my District well. I took it very seriously.

Before running for Office, I had been very successful as a business crisis consultant. I was contracted to enter very hostile environments, where emotions were running high, and pump life back into those dying businesses somehow. I had developed and honed signature techniques in these challenging environments, which had served these businesses very well over the years, such as "learn to respond, not react", "earn permission to be heard", and ironically, my personal favorite: **"you've lost the luxury of a meltdown".** ☺

I eventually narrowed my focus to entrepreneurial women, holding enchanting symposiums called Lady Like

Leaders, where I broadened the concepts around my signature techniques and proactively consulted women launching new businesses, helping them avoid the types of crises I was so accustomed to pulling businesses out of.

Like a pendulum, I have always swung between two main careers: consulting/speaking and professional songwriting. I covered my songwriting journey heavily in my first book, *Lady Up and Don't Quit*, if you'd like to fill in these blanks. But writing songs at the pro level is a world-class education in evoking emotions that move the needle in the human heart.

The epiphany was...

All my signature techniques that worked to help heal businesses in crisis, along with the emotional insight songwriting gave me, could have been applied to prevent the estrangement from my son and can be applied to the crisis of political division we find ourselves in today in families across America.

If only that had "clicked" sooner!

I ran my ideas by my dear friend and mentor, Dr. Ming Wang, who had written an insightful book with Dr. Rice Broocks during the pandemic called *Common Ground*. Universal Studios is about to release a movie about Dr. Wang's life and journey from communist China, facing labor camp for life, to graduating Harvard Medical School and MIT with honors.

He invented an incredible amniotic contact lens that has restored sight to millions of people around the world, but he focuses just as heavily in restoring sight to the spiritually blind in America in his philanthropic work. He was immediately on board and insisted on being the President of my Lady Up America Founders Club. How could I resist? I couldn't have been more honored.

I then pulled together a world-class BETA class to test my techniques and see if they truly did transfer to the political crisis in our relationships. They did. Then, I put them to the test with a tour of 18 battleground counties ahead of the 2022 Mid-Terms to see if they resonated in voter and political circles. They did.

The Lady Up America movement is a natural evolution of what I spent years learning, cultivating, teaching, and applying in crisis situations in business, as well as carefully observing what resonated with an audience as a professional songwriter. Now that I'm convinced these techniques transfer to the cultural struggles we are facing, I'm training Christian moms in them as fast as I can!

Running for State House of Representatives taught me a VERY powerful lesson: **there is no cavalry coming out of Washington**. Politics is downstream of culture. So, the power lies within us to win our culture back to God so that He can heal our land. Mastering the art of authentic emotional influence is the most effective way to gracefully win hearts and minds.

I hope what I've learned from my painful experience will prevent other moms from experiencing similar painful divisions in their relationships. I am on a mission to help moms become super influential around their dinner tables, neighborhoods, and communities.

We're in training now for the toughest spiritual battleground of our lifetime. With God's wind of favor at our back, and the techniques we master in this book, nothing shall be impossible! Let's Lady Up together and go win our country back!!!

Chapter Two

Is America Really a Christian Nation?

In today's "modern society", we've allowed people to convince us that it is not only unfashionable, but impolite to talk about our faith in public, in the workplace, in schools, or anywhere other than our Churches. As a result, we have downplayed our faith, or at least we think twice about what we share in mixed company. Afterall, we don't want to be impolite, unfashionable, or offensive. We want to be inclusive, open-minded, and certainly compassionate.

If we do have a moment of bravery to speak up about our faith, we hear pushbacks like, *"Don't push your religion on me"*. Never mind that their "religion" is being forced down our throats every waking minute. If we try to equate our cultural decline to our decline in Christian values, people throw out another pushback:

- *"We were NOT actually founded on Christian values."*

- *"How could a Christian nation allow slavery? "*

- *"There is a separation between Church and State".*

We don't know how to handle this pushback. We wonder if they are right? We struggle in our response to this because we aren't sure how to handle it, so we shrink back. I sure did, for years. But I'm about to prove to you that we were ABSOLUTELY founded on Christian Values.

This was the most eye-opening discovery for me, and it is foundational for Lady Up America. It gives us the solid rock to build every other technique upon and it will give you the confidence you need in tough discussions.

Our Founding Fathers warned us REPEATEDLY that the only way our Republic could sustain would be that we had to be trusted to be self-governing. Christian values were the moral compass for our Republic and the gauge for that self-governing process. Basically, the Bible was the gauge for right and wrong, and that the traditional/nuclear family was the best possible governing system. When I hear the scripture about how the fear of God is the beginning of wisdom, I understand that to mean that when we know God is always watching, and we have to ultimate answer to Him on judgment day, we learn to live for that audience of One.

When God is the spiritual authority over good men, then fathers can be trusted to be the spiritual authority in their homes, then moms yield to their husbands and to God out of that respect and reverence, but their opinions and insights are very valuable and have tremendous influence on their husbands, children, and communities. Godly families produced law-abiding, God-fearing citizens. Family is God's design and the best possible governing design for a sustainable country. What starts in the home spills out onto the streets of society, good or bad.

Our Founding Fathers wanted to limit the federal government in people's lives because they knew that it was like a monster. If government was kept small, we could tame it, but if it grew too large, it would devour us. We're certainly seeing that play out today. They were not insisting everyone "be" a Christian, in fact they were against oppressive religious laws because that's exactly what they were running from in a tyrannical King who imposed his religious beliefs on people.

But they knew we had to have one moral compass for society to sustain itself. Our common thread was the values of Christianity, and the hope was that people would share in it voluntarily because it held the framework for true and sustainable freedom.

If people had a reverence for God in their own homes and lives, they would govern themselves, accordingly, making it unnecessary for a large federal government. In the original 13 colonies, it was a requirement that you HAD to be a Christian to serve in Congress. I was fascinated to learn that, and it makes perfect sense. If you are in a position to make or change laws, and Christianity is the moral compass by which those laws are made, then you should be a Christian. That is common sense. Most of our Founding Fathers were devout Christians, and they knew that without obedience to God's natural law, genuine love for one another, and God's favor, that our freedom was unsustainable.

> *"Whatever may be conceded to the influence of refined education on minds of peculiar structure, reason and experience both forbid us to expect that National morality can prevail in exclusion of religious principle." - George Washington*

"Resistance to tyranny becomes the Christian and social duty of each individual. ...Continue steadfast and, with a proper sense of your dependence on God, nobly defend those rights which heaven gave, and no man ought to take from us." — John Hancock

"Now I will avow, that I then believed, and now believe, that those general Principles of Christianity, are as eternal and immutable, as the Existence and Attributes of God: and that those Principles of Liberty, are as unalterable as human Nature and our terrestrial, mundane System." — John Adams

For further proof that our country was founded in Christian principles, let's talk about the first American Bible. When we won our independence, the English King George cut us off from Bibles. In other words, he would not allow us to import them any longer. We began to run out, so Congress unprecedentedly approved and commissioned Robert Aitken, a publisher of our Journals of Congress, to print the first American Bible. They then sent out the Bible to every American as the moral compass by which to self-govern their lives. So, what about the pushback of "a separation between Church and State"? Well, would it surprise you to learn that no such statement exists in ANY of our founding documents or in our constitution? So then where did it come from? I'm so glad you asked! Thomas Jefferson was writing a letter to the Danbury Church assuring them that the government would stay out of "their" business.

"I contemplate with sovereign reverence that act of the whole American people which declared that their legislature should 'make no law respecting an establishment of religion, or prohibiting the free exercise thereof,' thus building a wall of separation between Church & State."

- Thomas Jefferson's Letter to the Baptist Association of Danbury, Connecticut,

January 1, 1802

The implication was that there would be a separation between "State and Church". Big difference there! Our Founding Fathers knew that the faith and political issues were intertwined, and all based on one moral compass of Christianity. You cannot have an "anything goes" society and expect it to sustain itself.

If people have differing opinions on what is right or wrong, who is the Umpire, if not God?

So, when people say things like "Morality shouldn't be legislated" my question is this: **What DO we legislate if not morality?**

Think about it…virtually every law is rooted in morality in some way. We are attempting to legislate what is right or fair. So, the next time you are faced with this pushback, I hope you feel more confident in your stance. America was absolutely founded in Christianity. Our only hope for a sustainable Republic is our return to it. It's as simple as that.

Chapter Three

What "Is" The Soul of Our Nation?

We often hear the opposing side make comments like, "We're fighting for the soul of our nation". What does that even mean? This is referring to the values of America, such as freedom, liberty, and the pursuit of happiness. But much like other common understandings of words and phrases, this one is being twisted and distorted for a political agenda in the most perverse ways possible.

Preying upon the emotions of Americans who have a vague-at-best understanding of our founding values, for political gain, is such a low road. But I must admit…I was one of those Americans up until 5 years ago.

I had NO idea what our founding values were, only a vague sense of what our country stood for. I did recite the Pledge of Allegiance back in elementary school, I took a few history classes, and I performed for some political rallies in my life, but that was about it. I was way too busy with the demands of my own life and didn't really see what any of that stuff had to do with me. It just wasn't my area, and I was fine with that.

I remember an early wakeup call when I was running for Office. I was asking one of my friends, Laura, for her vote. She said, "You've got my vote if you can answer this one question: are you a fiscal conservative?" I had never heard that term before, I had no idea how to answer her, and she probably saw that in my eyes. Shortly after that, I heard our Tennessee Senator Marsha Blackburn giving an interview and she made the statement: "*We conservatives believe in the rule of law*". Again, I had never heard that term before and I wanted to know where she got it.

I went on a hunt to find out what these two terms meant, and it eventually led me to what I'm about to show you. I couldn't believe what I found, and I remember thinking "*If only I had known about these sooner*". I felt they were so critically important that they should be shouted from rooftops and spoken into the hearts of every American. I couldn't believe how much they helped me understand our country so much more clearly and I couldn't believe I had never heard about them.

This is a game changing chapter.

Hold on to your hat! I am about to show you something that will instantly simplify ANY breaking news story. Additionally, with this tool, you can immediately get your bearings when the next political shock wave tries to throw us off our game. It thoroughly answers the question: *What "Is" The Soul of America?*

So let me set this up with something we can all likely relate to. Many of us are fans of HGTV's home renovation shows. One of my favorites is Ben and Erin Napier's *Hometown*. **Quick note here**: This show is set in Laural, Mississippi, the childhood home of our US Senator Marsha Blackburn as well. When she came on my Podcast, we had a fun conversation about it, where she took us down memory lane, and told stories about how her family knew Erin's. Check it out. But I digress.

One of the first things Ben & Erin identify, before they begin demolition, is the location of all load-bearing walls. They know that if they accidentally demo a load-bearing wall, the structure will no longer be sound, and the roof can cave in. What

I'm about to share with you I would like you to picture as the load-bearing walls of our country. There are 7 of them and they hold up the roof of our Republic. If one of these is knocked down, the roof can cave in.

They are called the **7 Core Principles of Conservatism**, which are the foundational principles for the Republican Party. They represent our identity, as Americans, or the soul of our nation. They can also be seen as our "True North" on America's compass, pointing us in the right direction when the storms of emotional confusion try and sweep us away. Let me first acknowledge that I know you may have a bad taste in your mouth about Republicans, but for the foreseeable future, warts and all, they are the conservative Party. Our job is to learn to elect better Republicans but stay with me for a few minutes because when you know these 7 values, then you can instantly find your way through political storms, emotional firestorms, and smokescreens. They will be foundational for voting in better Republicans, too!

I found these from US Congressman, Mike Johnson, when I first started building Lady Up America. He became our Speaker of the House in 2023. I am truly amazed by this divine connection, and I believe it is an indicator of God's hand in this.

So, before we learn all about them, we need a little context so that they make sense.

Our Founding Fathers had a massive responsibility in trying to set us up for success. Many brave people sacrificed their fortunes and their lives on bloody battlefields to stand together and secure our freedom. We have heard these words all our lives, but I want to take a moment to imagine the scene and honor the kind of bravery they displayed. Here is one of my favorite quotes from George Washington when he readied himself and his army for a seemingly impossible and crucial battle on the Delaware river, in a blinding snowstorm on Christmas Day:

"The fate of unborn millions will now depend, under God, on the courage and conduct of this army. Our cruel and unrelenting enemy leaves us only the choice of brave resistance, or the most abject submission. We have, therefore, to resolve to conquer or die." — George Washington

Think about how bitter cold it was for these men in raggedy clothes and worn-out shoes in Delaware near an icy river. They didn't have the King's war chest to finance their side of this war. When their shoes finally fell apart from marching hundreds of miles, they wrapped scraps of fabric around their feet and kept going, in snow and ice! The enemy often tracked them by their bloody footprints. Many died of frostbite.

And yet, they were THAT determined to stand up for freedom for their generation and for ours. None of us, I hope, will ever have to sacrifice at that level. They did all of that to win us our freedom. Our job is to maintain it and never hand it over, out of honor and respect to them. God rest their souls.

George Washington explained that the snowstorm on that crucial battlefield, although harsh, turned out to be the favor of God. First, it caused the enemy to relax a bit, thinking that our army wouldn't advance in such weather. Then, when they did advance, the wind blew towards the enemy. So, it blew snow and wind into their faces, disorienting them, and giving our men another advantage. George Washington ended up praising God for the advantages and the divine blessings he watched play out on the battlefield that day as they earned their win.

To have displayed THAT level of bravery and come THAT far at such an incredible cost, and now be faced with the monumental job of establishing the right governmental structure to maintain it for centuries to come…I just can't imagine the pressure. Keep in mind that there has never been a story like America's in human history. Against innumerable odds, with the favor of God as the only explanation, the American experiment of freedom and self-governance was born.

So, our Founding Fathers really wanted to get this right. They studied other governments to see what brought them down so that they could protect us from that same fate. They studied the Roman government, the Greek government, the writings of Socrates, etc. When they came out of the deliberation room of the Constitutional Convention, they were asked, what kind of government we now have. The answer, from Benjamin Franklin was, *"A Republic, if we can keep it."*

These 7 conservative values are woven throughout our Declaration of Independence, Constitution, and Bill of Rights. They are foundational for our entire Republic. They are brilliant because they are non-partisan, non-divisive, and agreeable to almost everyone when they hear them. They represent the intention at the founding of our country, which was to set us up for the best possible success and protect our Republic from crumbling like other governments had done.

The 7 Core Principles of Conservatism

Paraphrased from US Representative Mike Johnson via his website: https://mikejohnson.house.gov/7-core-principles-of-conservatism

Limited Government - The bigger the government, the smaller our individual liberties. A legitimate government operates only by the consent of the governed and is more efficient and less corrupt when it is limited in its size & scope. Our Constitution provides important safeguards against government encroachment, a vital separation of powers, and a necessary system of checks and balances.

Biggest Take-A-Way: The bigger the government, the less free we are.

Individual Freedom - In America, we proclaim the self-evident truths that all of us are created equal and granted by God the same inherent freedoms, such as the natural and unalienable rights to life, liberty, and the ability to pursue happiness, our own

property, to build wealth and defend ourselves and our families. The purpose of government is to secure these rights, not grant them. Big difference! **Biggest Take-a-Way: God gives us our rights and our value, not government.**

Human Dignity - Because all men are created equal and in the image of God, every human life has dignity and value, and every person should be measured only by the content of their character. A just government protects life, honors marriage, and family as the primary institutions of a healthy society and embraces the vital cultural influences of religion and morality. Public policy should always encourage education and emphasize the virtue of hard work as a pathway out of poverty, while public assistance programs should be reserved only for those who are truly in need.

Biggest Take-a-Way: We have dignity and value because God created us, and everyone should aim to honor God with their life and their work.

Fiscal Responsibility - Congress has a moral and constitutional duty to be good stewards of our money, to resolve the current debt crisis, bring spending under control, balance the federal budget, reform, and modernize entitlement programs, eliminate fraud, waste, and abuse, pursue continued pro-growth tax reforms, and permanent tax reductions, and restore regular order and accountability in the budget and appropriations processes.

Biggest Take-a-Way: The government doesn't make or produce anything. They are stewards over our money.

Rule of Law - Ours is "a government of laws and not of men," and the rule of law is our foundation. To maintain ordered liberty and a civilized society, public and private virtue should be encouraged, and justice must be administered equally and impartially to all. Each branch of government must adhere to the Constitution and Congress must provide oversight.

Biggest Take-a-Way: What is good for the goose should be good for the gander.

Free Markets - The free enterprise system rewards hard work and self-sacrifice and is the basis and genius of the American economy. The government often stands as the greatest obstacle to the progress and prosperity of free people. Free markets and free trade agreements allow for innovation, improvement and economic expansion as risk-takers are given the liberty to pursue the American dream and create more jobs and upward mobility for more people.

Biggest Take-a-Way: If you walk into a produce section of a grocery store in the middle of a New York winter and have options, that is a result of Free Markets.

Peace Through Strength - The first obligation of the federal government is to provide for the "common defense" of the US by protecting our homeland and our strategic interests abroad. Because America serves as moral leadership in an increasingly dangerous world, and weakness invites aggression, we must remain the strongest military power on earth fully prepared and

26

capable of defeating any adversaries, tyrants, or terrorists, under any circumstances, at any time.

Biggest Take-a-Way: Government's #1 job is to keep us safe.

So, now that you have seen these, how does it make you feel? The first time I saw this, it instantly brought everything into focus. It helped me understand how to make sense of news cycles. It gave me a gauge to hold policies up against and instantly see how they stack up. It gives me a measuring stick, other than emotion, by which to formulate my opinion on topics or make a selection in a voting booth.

No matter what the political hot topic is in tonight's news cycle, they all root back to ONE of these 7 Values. Every single one!!! The border crisis is rooted in Peace Through Strength. Abortion is rooted in Human Dignity. The out-of-control spending in Washington is rooted in Fiscal Responsibility.

The *SOUL OF AMERICA* is no longer a point of confusion. It is crystal clear. These 7 values are our true north in navigating the politically confusing storms of our day. These are the load-bearing walls of our country. For those trying to knock down our load-bearing walls, we must take the hammer out of their hands.

Chapter Four

Modernizing Our Approach

$\mathcal{P}$eople with opposing views love to argue that our 7 founding values are old-fashioned and have nothing to do with us in our modern day, like how I used to think. But I'm about to explain how they are NOT and how what happened back then matters VERY much to our lives today!

Just as George Washington knew on that Christmas Day in the snowstorm, we must have the favor of God in our efforts if we are to hope for any victory for our country. America's values never go out of style or expire because they are rooted in God's word, which is timeless. The human spirit never changes. There is nothing new under the sun. Over the centuries, there have always been and always will be human frailties like selfishness, greed, lying, cheating, bullying, worrying, the inner quest for purpose, the need to be loved, the desire for respect, etc.

Likewise, God never changes. He has always been and always will be patient, forgiving, merciful, and loving towards His children who love Him. He is also a God of justice. For those who mocked Him, perverted His great love for us, and insisted on being their own god, it never ended well. He is the same yesterday, today, and tomorrow. So, with our country founded in His word and laws, they stand the test of time, and they are rock solid.

Yet, we do need to learn to bring these TIMELESS values into modern conversation if we hope to win over the new generation. The values don't change, but the way we frame them should. We can start with not using words like "get back to" or "return" in our conversation. This will lessen the feeling that we are returning to something old or going "backwards" - even though we know what I just described to be true.

I just gave you the example of HGTV's Hometown, so let's use that. Here is a statement I often make in mixed company:

"Our founding values are the load bearing walls of our country and we've got to take the hammer out of the hands of those trying to knock them down." — Diane Canada

This is a way we can modernize our approach, rather than coming across like we're trying to take the country backwards by returning to something old and irrelevant for today's modern age.

Another thing we must do is lighten up! I'm not recommending we diminish the seriousness of the situation, but we have got to lose the intensity in our approach, or we drive them away and never have the chance to win them over. I know this seems counterintuitive, which is often the case when we walk out faith.

For instance, when we are really worried about a situation in our lives, God instructs us to cast our cares on Him and then go be of service to someone else. We really struggle with that. Instead, we carry a vibe of intensity, we justify binge eating, we roll it over and over in our minds all day, we call everybody we know to bounce it off them, just sure that we will eventually come up with a way to fix it. But, in my experience, we end up only making the situation worse.

However, when I give it to God and then go help somebody else, it takes my mind off my own troubles for a while and God works behind the scenes to bring about the ideal solution. There's a calm in this approach that boggles people's minds. They'll say things like, "*How can you not be stressed out right now*?" They are impressed with our ability to enjoy life while we're waiting on God to tell us what's next. He may not reveal the next step on my timetable, or in the way that I was hoping for, but His solution is perfect, nonetheless.

God whispers wisdom in our hearts, He never shouts. We need to carve out moments of being still so that we can hear His whisper. He shouldn't have to compete with the noise in our heads or in the world to be heard. His voice should take priority. I often hear Him best when I turn off the radio in the car, when I'm walking in nature or sitting on my porch in the sunshine without distractions.

Many people wonder what God's voice sounds like if they have yet to hear it for themselves. For me, it's a gentle statement that I hear in my mind. It's crystal clear, there's no mistaking that it is Him. His tone is parental, loving, and he speaks with authority. He will ask me to do things that take me completely out of my comfort zone, which has caused me to argue with Him or beg Him not to make me do it over the years. I have matured enough in my faith now that I don't argue anymore, I just obey quicker, because I trust Him more now. I go into a lot more detail about some of my experiences with Him like this in my first book, *Lady Up and Don't Quit*. If you decide to read it, look for the part where he gives me a very uncomfortable directive during a women's retreat, and how that act of obedience ended up spanning 7 years and ended up on television. It was a rather profound experience. His voice is always in alignment with His word. He never tells us to do anything that would contradict the Bible and there is incredible reward for obeying Him.

The truth is that being in your Bible every day, learning to listen for God's whisper of wisdom, and then obeying Him is where the peace is. At the end of the day, I realized that worrying is selfish because it keeps "me" on my mind all day and helps nobody. I've found some humor and comfort in admitting that I'm just not smart enough to run my own life. I have gotten very comfortable with leaving it in God's capable hands, doing what He asks, serving others, and just trusting that He's hard at work behind the scenes of my life. It gets easier the more we do it, but it's hard at first.

So, in that same spirit, the energy we bring to a conversation is incredibly important to our ability to influence. People pick up on fear, desperation, and anger, even if we are saying all the right things. Our demeanor or tone gives us away. We've got to calm down and align our own hearts and minds with God's word so that we genuinely come across in an appealing way towards those we want to influence. We need to realize that the fate of America is in God's hands, not ours, which helps us to release the outcome. This takes all the pressure off. This madness in our culture is no surprise to Him and only He can turn it around. We do our part, and He does his. But I must remind myself all the time that the outcome is not up to me, it's up to the person and to God.

Even those who are in charge were allowed to be by Him for some bigger purpose. Look at how the unfolding events of the 2020 Presidential election season motivated the Church! In Jesus's day, there was a very corrupt government, the Roman Empire. Jesus entered history and could have destroyed it, but instead, He taught us how to have peace and joy among it. In other words, He didn't remove us from tough circumstances, but taught us to thrive in the middle of them. So, we need a constant reminder that the JOY of the Lord is our STRENGTH! Not fear, anger, or frustration.... but the JOY!!!

It's very hard to interrupt the momentum of worry, fear, frustration, and anger, but we must admit it is not helpful. I heard someone say that worry is like a rocking chair; we're busy all day but we aren't going anywhere. JOY, however, is a quiet contentment. Releasing the outcome helps us to relax into these conversations and that is VERY attractive to people...and a LOT more effective towards our ultimate goal of influencing them! We end up achieving, much more often, the very thing we hoped to achieve when we release the temptation to force it.

Whether people want to be, or not, they are drawn to light. Be that light. Evil hates it, but the people we want to reach will gravitate towards it. They are desperately looking for hope in this dark world, even those who behave poorly sometimes. They are drawn to warmth and light! So, please, radiate that light!

Chapter Five

Clarity Among the Confusion

C onfusion is a war tactic. Redefining words, reassigning genders, and trying to normalize the perverse, are very purposeful confusion tactics. Our current culture is taking gas lighting to a whole new level. Here's a quote from an age-old book, The Art of War:

> *"The whole secret lies in confusing the enemy,*
> *so that he cannot fathom our real intent."*
> *– Sun Tzu*

Confusion can cause the enemy to surrender before the battle even begins. We see this playing out in our culture rampantly. Because so many of us are unaware of what the Biblical stance is on today's cultural hot topics, explanations behind things that don't quite sit well with our soul can sound reasonable. I heard a great line from a movie one time that said, *"People don't drink the sand because they're thirsty. They drink the sand because they don't know the difference."*

If we ask any questions or disagree, we risk being accused of racism, homophobia, or a host of other "isms". So, some of us find it easier to comply behind slogans like *"live and let live"*, *"we shouldn't judge"*, and *"love is love"*.

So many well-meaning Christians are complying, thinking that loving people not only means we accept them, but we should affirm them. We even hear this coming from Church pulpits across America, teaching their congregations that Jesus was all about love as a way to rationalize their complicity and affirmation.

We do have a few brave Pastors across our country who are not bowing the knee to woke culture and, instead, standing strong for God's word. Some of my favorites, who I learn a LOT from, are Pastor Allen Jackson of World Outreach Church in Murfreesboro, TN, my former Pastor Aaron Davis, and my wonderful current Pastor John Richardson. They are speaking truth, in love, unapologetically. Yes, Jesus is love, but there's a LOT more to His character and teaching then group hugs, as Pastor Allen would say.

We're being hit with one radical ideology after another targeting our children, at a scale that's hard to absorb, and it is all very purposeful. We're exhausted from the overwhelm. We don't want to be ostracized. We don't like confrontation. So, for some, it's easier to just comply. Afterall, what choice do we have, right? This complicity is demanded now in the public square. The forces demanding it seem very powerful. It seems like they are large in number, but they are not. The few just hold the levers of power. Much like the man behind the curtain in the Wizard of Oz, it's all a big show.

It seems like Christians are the minority, but there are SO many more of us than there are of them in the United States. America is still a Christian-dominated nation, but if they can convince us that Christianity is no longer thriving or wanted, then like that quote says, we will surrender before the battle begins. Well, not on my watch we won't!!!

Christianity is under serious attack, as is the Jewish faith. Why such hatred towards Christians and Jews? I did a LOT of study in this area, and I got some unsettling answers. There is a major push towards Marxism in our country right now, but it's not new, it's simply the closest to fruition that it's ever been. This push has been going on for the last several generations and it is hiding under the guise of Socialism, but I have learned that those two words are interchangeable. In other words, they result in the same outcome.

A lot of our young people are being seduced by the idea of Socialism in our universities, especially. Marxist professors and instructors have been infiltrating our school system and colleges for decades because they know if they can help shape the minds of our young people early, then they won't have to fight those who know better. It's basically easier to shape them than fight them.

These professors and instructors come in with fancy pedigrees and convince students that proper Socialism just hasn't been tried correctly yet. They tug on their heart strings with the idea that in the richest country in the world, everyone should have equal access to everything and that no one should struggle. But these unsuspecting young minds have no idea the monster they are awakening. Ronald Reagan had a great quote about it. He said,

"'Socialism only works in two places: Heaven where they don't need it and hell where they already have it.'"

— Ronald Reagan

They are now looking to the government to provide equity and are becoming more and more willing to yield to the government. What they don't realize is that a government that can give you everything can also take it away. And history has shown repeatedly that they will. Surrendering our power to the government in exchange for them taking care of us will never end well, no matter how well-intentioned the people are. It never has. It never will. Again, human nature doesn't change. That is one *"I told you so"* that none of us want to say. Once freedom is handed over, the only way to ever get it back is bloody.

I have come to learn the necessity of pain and struggle in our lives. When people choose a positive pathway out of it, it produces many great things. It awakens our ability to be creatively resourceful, it develops integrity and humility, it gives us the opportunity to see what we're made of and a sense of dignity in accomplishment, the chance to enjoy the fruits of our labor, and such a deeper intimacy and trust in God. It's so very sad to deprive people of these things, and their God-given purpose, by convincing them they need to be taken care of by government and shouldn't be expected to endure anything negative, hard, or critical.

When I was growing up, I had an incredible opportunity to see the contrast between the wealthy ruling class and the poor. I spent the early part of my life in the Church, as my father was a Pastor, until he walked out on my mom, my sister and I for another woman when I was 8 years old. After he left, my mom took a job as a Governess for an affluent family in Atlanta.

My mom went from being the Pastor's wife to scrubbing floors and helping raise someone else's kids for a living. This taught me about resiliency, resourcefulness, and humility. My mom could have easily accepted a welfare check and food stamps because Lord knows we qualified, but she chose hard work instead. I'm grateful for that because she set an important example.

The silver lining was that, due to the nature of her job, my sister and I basically grew up with their children. We spent all our Spring, Summer, and Fall school breaks with this family. We would spend weekends there housesitting and taking care of the kids while the parent's traveled. We would spend all day by the pool with their kids at their Country Club and then we'd come home to our small apartment with very little in the cupboards.

I remember one night mom divided our last can of Campbells's chicken noodle soup between my sister and me. I asked her what she was going to eat, and she said, *"Oh, I'm not hungry, honey, you two eat."* I remember going to bed hungry, so often, but I never said a word because I knew she was hungrier. These experiences built all kinds of character in not only us, but the children she helped raise. They are still very close to our family to this day, and we all learned valuable lessons from my mother. Things haven't been easy, but I wouldn't give anything in the world for those masterclasses in life.

I once heard a story about how a man sat down on a park bench and noticed a butterfly struggling to break free from its cocoon. The man felt sorry for the little thing and helped him open the cocoon and break free. What he didn't realize was that the butterfly needed that struggle because it helped release fluid from its body into the wings and develop the strength to be able to fly once it is out of the cocoon. Without that struggle, the butterfly's wings are underdeveloped, and it will die. So, struggle is not something we should avoid. It is a necessary part of survival, building character, and reaching our purpose.

I do want to touch on one other important thing. There has been a growing trend of disrespect in our culture, especially between newer and previous generations.

I looked up the Brittanica definition and found this:

"A feeling of admiring someone or something that is good, valuable, important, etc."

- www.britannica.com/dictionary/respect

I think this is where we are getting tripped up among generational gaps because we don't share the same perspective on what is *good, valuable, or important*. So, we admire different things causing a breakdown in respect.

In the GenX generation and before, we admired parents, teachers, elders, veterans, etc. because we valued these people, and they were important to us. Save some bad eggs here and there, they provided for us and were looking out for our well-being, their wisdom from experience was valuable as was their approval, and they paved important roads for us that we are now walking on into brighter futures. It seems that what many people value or find importance in today does not always look like that, especially if they didn't come from a Christian home.

Many young people today value social media likes and celebrities simply because they're rich and famous, not because they've achieved anything significant. They do think there are important social causes out there, but they lack the context or perspective for those causes, so even though they really mean well, they are often deeply deceived. Many of them don't see value in wisdom from people who have life experience, and they are extremely fragile emotionally, and they just want to figure things out for themselves. I say, let's capitalize on that. Stay tuned.

If we look back over Generation X, the Baby Boomers, and even back to the Greatest Generation before them, we can trace the trends that helped us arrive here to today's generation. In the Greatest Generation, they were tough as nails because they had to survive extremely difficult challenges, like the Great Depression or World War II for instance. They didn't have much time to consider anybody's feelings because they were always in survival mode.

The Baby Boomers were a result of all those soldiers coming home from war and starting families while enjoying great economic prosperity in America, but they were also conditioned for stability. They were children of war heroes and survivors of the Great Depression, so they had thick skin, too. The motto, *suck it up, Buttercup*, comes to mind.

My generation, GenX, interacted regularly with the Greatest Generation because they were our grandparents, so they tried to toughen us up and we learned a lot of great lessons from them. But the Baby Boomers ushered in changes in our culture, which proved consequential. My generation was the first to be impacted by the breakdown of the family with rampant divorce, a massive relaxation of traditional values, movies and music that celebrated promiscuity, and faith becoming MIA in our homes. We weren't sure what was right or wrong, especially when our parents made statements like, *"Do as I say, not as I do."*

Single moms found it hard to make it on their own, so they ended up in multiple marriages, bringing challenging stepparent dynamics, and homes unintentionally became emotional battlefields. We were the latchkey kids, coming home to empty homes, which taught us to be very independent. Our parents believed kids were resilient and there wasn't much money or need for therapy. Therapy was frowned upon in my generation, much differently than in today's culture. We had a lot of emotions that we didn't know how to handle because of instability in our homes and the variety of dynamics we were trying to navigate.

I remember feeling very confused and easily upset. I was told things like, *"You're just too sensitive."* and *"You need thicker skin.*" So, we just learned how to deal, the best we could. I coped with the emotional battlefield in my home by staying gone as much as possible and filling my time with excusable reasons to not be home. I got heavily involved in color guard, where we had long practices, games, and lots of competitions out of town. I also took a part-time job at Sears Portrait Studio and babysat as much as possible for our neighbors. Many of us from GenX learned that working hard was an emotional escape and, although not the healthiest coping skill, it did develop an incredible work ethic.

I'm going to take a short detour here to share this personal story because it is relevant to one of the 7 values we discussed earlier, Human Dignity. While on the color guard, I was the drill team captain, spun flags and rifles. Our rifle instructor, Richard, was an incredible black man who had marched and taught the Spirit of Atlanta DCI (Drum and Bugle Corps International) color guard. They are mind-blowingly good!!! I highly encourage you to Google them.

Richard would keep us on the field to practice, long into the evening, after the marching band had gone home. We used those heavy white wooden rifles with black straps on the bottom. He wanted our spins to be in unison, the height of our tosses to be exact, and for us to be so sharp that when the rifle hit our

45

hands, he could hear only one click from the straps. He wouldn't let us go home until he saw and heard that. We would be in agonizing pain, so tired, and ready to hit him. He would see our anger and raise it by saying, "*I got aaaaaaaaall night.*" We learned to channel our anger productively and achieve the goal so we could go home.

He taught us to push past physical and mental barriers, to perform from a deeper level, and the payoff felt incredible. I remember when our buses would pull up into these huge competitions, I could hear people whispering, "*Oh, no…Norcross High School is here.*" He had T-shirts made for us that read, "*We're not here for the competition…we ARE the competition.*" We swept almost every single competition we participated in, and nobody was more animated than Richard in the stands cheering for us.

He always brought an air horn, and we would listen for it from the field the moment our show ended. We knew if we heard the air horn in the stands, that Richard was proud. He pushed us because he loved us and wanted us to feel the exhilaration of earning the win. There was a healthy pride I learned in hard work that I carry with me to this day. I want everyone to have a chance to feel that payoff. Anyway, back on track.

GenX then raised the Millennials where we wanted to give them everything we wished we would have had as kids, especially when it came to nurturing their emotions. Most of us had no idea how to make good choices for our own lives, so we, too, ended up complicating things further with divorces of our own, multiple marriages, stepchildren dynamics, etc. We knew we had caused our kids the same pain we felt as kids, so we wrapped them in bubble wrap, coddled them, and tried to prevent them from ever having struggle a day in their life.

We catered to their feelings, bought them lots of stuff, and we tried to be their friend instead of their parent. We tapped back into our favorite coping mechanism, which was to bury our pain in hard work. We were high achieving workaholics. We were a hot mess. Our Millennial kids were the first to play with hand-held gaming devices, the internet came on the scene in their generation, and they learned how to entertain themselves while we were busy working. I can understand how many of them resented our work.

They have far fewer coping skills for the struggles of life than we had. So many are on anti-depressants, suicide rates are extremely high, they are afraid to get drivers licenses, and they are very reluctant to leave home. Many have been heavily influenced by woke college professors, CRT helped shape them as it was going on in schools right under our noses, so their values seem a Grand Canyon apart from ours. They see us as hypocrites and oftentimes even toxic to their worldview, as many of us realize that a return to traditional values is our only hope. We see how far the country has gone off the rails because we had a reference point in the Greatest Generation. They don't have that reference point. As they start families of their own, raising GenZ, they want to expose their kids to alternative family structures and a set of values we cannot relate to. They see themselves as the evolved ones and they see traditional viewpoints as toxic and oppressive. How can we blame them?

When we want to blame CRT, blame the government, blame Hollywood, etc., I say we need to blame the one in the mirror, especially if you are from my generation X. We did this!!! This lays at our feet. While we were trying to cope with our own traumas, justifying our coping mechanisms, our spiritual negligence created the void that our kids were swallowed up in. The church is a joke to them. We can't win them by espousing how "right" we are…we've lost all credibility…we must win them by telling them how "wrong" we've been, apologizing, and humbling ourselves to God and to them. We have left our children vulnerable to those who would insidiously feast on their emotional fragility. We created a breeding ground for Marxism. Yes, we certainly had help from the government, Hollywood, big tech, etc. But the silence from the church is what is ushering in Marxism.

Here is the abbreviated bedrock of Marxism, from my understanding, after reading the Communist Manifesto from Karl Marx and Friedrich Engels and then deepening my understanding of it from Kimberly Ell's book, *The Invincible Family* (which I HIGHLY recommend):

Marxist Agenda

- ✓ **God must be removed as an authority figure.**
- ✓ **Dads must come out of the home as authority figures.**

    The strong bond between mother and child must be severed so that mothers are no longer necessary.

    Children must belong to the State.

2 of these 4 boxes are checked. With all 4 boxes checked, true Marxism can flourish. With just a quick glance around our cultural staples, it's obvious they are working very hard on the 3rd step of severing the bond between mothers and their children, as well as making mothers no longer necessary for society. We see women being referred to now as "birthing people", as well as

numerous other indicators that they want moms out of the way and for the State to have full control over our kids. Moms are the final barrier to state control of our kids.

If you want the chilling end-game goals for State control over our kids, please read Kimberly's book I mentioned above. It is very objective and balanced but has fact-based answers on "why" they are oversexualizing our kids in elementary school and that that State control will mean for pedophilia. I'm telling you, it's chilling. Sympathetic messaging is the Marxist's preferred war tactic of confusion; the idea that *"We Care And "They" Don't."* This tactic basically implies that if you really care about people and want to make sure that wealth is distributed equitably, then Marxism is the best way to govern. But here's the cold hard truth that most countries find out the hard way:

Marxism doesn't distribute wealth,
It distributes poverty.

I had a wonderful conversation with a woman named Daniella who grew up in Marxist Romania. You can find our full episode on my Podcast Channel, Lady Up America. I wanted to understand the day-to-day ways that Marxism affected families and individuals. I asked her to give me personal stories that she remembered. She was generous in doing so. Here are two that really stood out in my mind.

She first told me about how the government would distribute vouchers to go to the grocery store and get your rationed food items for the week. But she explained that she and her grandfather would often go together, and they had to wait in long lines, for hours and hours, to get their turn to shop.

She visibly had tears in her eyes when she told me this. When they got their turn, there was nothing left to buy but scraps. There were still many people behind them in line. So, it wasn't that they didn't have the money to shop, there just wasn't enough supply to meet the demand.

She then told me something I'll never forget. She said that if you were elderly, around 65 or older, and you started to have a heart attack or needed emergency medical attention, the ambulance would not come for you. The government saw you as someone no longer contributing to society, disposable, so they would simply let you die on your own with no medical attention.

It was heartbreaking. She said one of the other contributing factors was that there was a major shortage of doctors, especially good doctors, because there was no incentive for them to spend half their life in medical school for little reward. She also said that because of the lack of competition in Hospitals the conditions were extremely unsanitary and often just downright gross. She said that she and her family would hope and pray they didn't get sick because they didn't want to have to go to such nasty hospitals.

These are the things young people who advocate for Marxism and Socialism don't know to consider. They truly believe in their hearts that they are compassionately doing what is right. The sympathetic messaging the Progressive Left sends to America is that they are so much more compassionate than those hard-hearted conservatives. Nothing could be further from the truth. Conservatives know that Progressives are luring well-meaning people into a dangerously deceptive web and the spider will eventually bite. But we never get the opportunity to show them that if we never get the chance to influence them. They just think we are fear mongering and they tune us out.

So, when we allow fear, anger, and frustration for this lost generation to drive us, then we play right into that messaging because we do come across as unhinged and hard-hearted. We literally make their case for them with bad behavior that they can point to and say, *"See, they don't care about you. We do."* It's an age-old tactic the enemy has used for centuries. Again, there is nothing really new under the sun. But why should he change the tactic? It has always worked in the past on numerous generations.

As Christians, we know what REAL love and compassion looks like, from Jesus Christ, and we truly do want the VERY best for this generation. It breaks our hearts that they can't see through this deception.

We know that this confusing message they send out to the masses paints us in the most unflattering light, but it is simply a war tactic, and a very effective one at that. Jesus NEVER forfeited the TRUTH for compassion but taught us that the most compassionate thing we can do is speak truth. It is not compassionate to go along with a lie, coddle the sense of oppression, or normalize the perverse, especially because it has eternal consequences. We must speak TRUTH, IN LOVE always. It takes massive amounts of courage to do this, which is why we need Him to help us with that.

Cancel culture is not new. In Jesus's day, cancel culture was much harsher. If you went against the Pharisees or the Roman rulers, it meant death, and a brutal one. There were major consequences for following Jesus. In our culture, we think it's terrible to be mocked, fired, or ostracized from our friend groups.

Think about the degree of courage it took for the Disciples to take a stand in their day. Their cancel culture makes ours look like child's play. Ask God to give you discernment so that you can see through the fog of confusion going forward...ask Him for His wisdom to keep you from being deceived. And ask Him for courage to speak truth, in love, as He guides you to.

Chapter Six

Stepping Into Your Power

N ow that we have clarity about the enemy's tactic, and the consequences of allowing him to gain territory in the hearts and minds of well-meaning people, we can work smarter. It's time to learn how to step into our power! We have no power on our own, apart from God, but in Him we have tremendous power and authority. Most of us just don't know how to access it.

Many of us have been praying profusely for our kids and our country and wondering why our prayers aren't working. Some of us are just laying down because it all seems futile. I am sure the Israelites thought it was futile as they stood between the Red Sea and the approaching Egyptian army. Some of us believe we are in the end times and it's better to just inconspicuously mind our p's and q's until Jesus comes back. He commands us to fear not. That doesn't mean we won't feel fear, it just means we are not to bow to it. If He does come back soon, don't you want Him to catch you at bat, swinging for the rafters, rather than biting your nails in the dugout? Think about it.

Our kids and our grandkids provide our motivation to lady up and not quit. Since this is a spiritual battle between good and evil in our culture, and not really a political one, we've got to learn to fight with spiritual weapons.

Before we get into the details, I want to make a couple of declarations to ease our minds from last chapter. First off, the enemy will never succeed in separating mothers from their kids, not indefinitely. God connected us in very special ways to our children, chemically and emotionally. Our children may get angry at us, but they will always crave a relationship with us, just as we will with them.

God designed that bond, and it is unbreakable in the heart. That love remains, and it wins out over every enemy attack, eventually. There is nothing more powerful than a mother's love or her prayer for her children. So, pray over your child in a powerful way:

- "I thank you Lord that no weapon formed against my child shall prosper. Thank you, angels, for your hedge of protection around him."
- "I thank you, Lord, that you are a God of restoration, and you are restoring my child to me, in Jesus's name."
- "I command you, Satan, to take your hands off my child, in the name of Jesus Christ. Flee from him."

These are powerful prayers we can pray as mothers, but we can also pray in the same way over all the precious children of America.

If we feel our prayers aren't working, we need to ask ourselves 3 hard questions:

1. Am I being disobedient to God in any area of my life?

2. Am I holding onto any unforgiveness?

3. Am I vulnerable to spiritual attacks?

These things hinder our ability to walk out our power and authority, which also hinder our ability to authentically influence. We've got to course correct!

Here are the ways we step into our full spiritual authority and power:

Obedience

We're going to get into this deeper in our next chapter but let me touch on it here. If we truly want to experience the power we inherited from Jesus in this world, and have God's full favor, then we absolutely must be in obedience. It's not easy, but it is necessary. And, like other things we've already discussed, it gets easier with time and practice.

Obedience means walking in God's definition of love, not the worlds. Love is not a feeling, it's an action. It also means following His commandments and walking out the fruit of the spirit. I'll cover that heavily in the next chapter. You're going to LOVE it, I promise!!! ☺

Forgiveness

I got stuck on this step for most of my life. I thought that forgiving someone was like me saying that what they did to me was okay; that somehow, they were going to skate and never have to pay for what they did. I was wrong. It just means that I choose to let go of my idea of justice, and to trust God's.

I didn't realize that holding onto that unforgiveness was like drinking poison and hoping the other person would die. It only hurt me and held me back from God's purpose from my life.

We hate the thought of praying for our enemies, and we are so resistant to doing it, but God commands that. It's not negotiable. We just need to understand what it means and why God would ask such a monumental task of us. We need to understand His character a bit better.

Part of the Lord's prayer is "forgive us of our trespasses, as we forgive those who have trespassed against us". I've come to learn that everything we experience in life, even horrible things inflicted on us by other people's free will or even things God takes away, can be worked for good. It doesn't mean that what happened to us was good, at all. It just means that God turns ashes into beauty when we trust Him, and your mess becomes your message.

That is SO hard to do initially. We are hard-wired for justice in our minds and hearts. We don't feel like we can move on until the scales are balanced again. God has taught me, through many tears, to release the outcome of even the most awful injustices because I can trust Him with it. I've been walking with the Lord long enough now, over 30 years, that I've learned His character and how He spiritually redeems.

It's different than how the world does. The valleys we go through are where we grow in intimacy with Him, it's where we learn to trust Him, and it's where He purifies our motives. Maybe

59

I'll write a book on that next, but for today, I encourage you to trust Him and obey Him about forgiveness.

I had a dear friend walk me through and teach me how to forgive many people in my life in the most incredible way. His name is Javier Peña, and I am forever grateful to him for helping me get unstuck in this area. I had no idea I was carrying so much emotional weight. He uses music in surprising and profound ways in his technique. It's extraordinary.

Javier has an entire program on walking women through the art of forgiveness. It is gentle, deep, a bit painful at first, but SO worth it on the other side. The beauty is that once you do it correctly, you are free, and you don't have to carry that weight anymore. I did this process a year and a half before writing this book and I'm still free. The pain doesn't come back, you are done with it.

I couldn't recommend Javier highly enough. You can learn more here: **javierpena.net.** Give yourself the biggest gift and forgive those who have hurt you and don't forget to add yourself to the list. You've beat yourself up long enough.

Spiritual Armor

Ephesians 6:10-18 is our foundation for this third step. Here is the scripture:

10 Finally, be strong in the Lord and in his mighty power. 11 Put on the full armor of God, so that you can take your stand against the devil's schemes. 12 For our struggle is not against flesh and blood, but against the rulers, against the authorities, against the powers of this dark world and against the spiritual forces of evil in the heavenly realms. 13 Therefore put on the full armor of God, so that when the day of evil comes, you may be able to stand your ground, and after you have done everything, to stand. 14 Stand firm then, with the belt of truth buckled around your waist, with the breastplate of righteousness in place, 15 and with your feet fitted with the readiness that comes from the gospel of peace. 16 In addition to all this, take up the shield of faith, with which you can extinguish all the flaming arrows of the evil one. 17 Take the helmet of salvation and the sword of the Spirit, which is the word of God.

- Ephesians 6:10-18

A lot of people really struggle with the idea that there is such a thing as a spiritual battle. I did for years. I just didn't get that, and I felt like people were a little too "out there" in their faith when I would hear them bring it up. I saw these people as religious zealots that I needed to steer clear of, for sure.

I told you about my homelife being upended, to say the least, when my dad left us for another woman. We fell very far away from our faith for years because of that and it has been a hard road back for me. People talk about *church hurt* and I had that in spades, as you can imagine. If anyone should have a seemingly good excuse to blow off Christianity, I suppose it would be me. I mean, my dad was a PASTOR!!! That's not supposed to happen in the Pastor's family.

So, on this road back, I had major trust issues when it came to God. I was very cautious about what I've allowed myself to believe. I had all kinds of filters to sift through over the years. Even when I gave my heart to the Lord in a friend's living room after an incredibly painful experience in 1992, I had a lot of growing up in the faith to do. Again, I open up about that a lot in my first book, *Lady Up and Don't Quit*.

As I said before, God has the best drip campaign, ever! He guides us lovingly, slowly, and methodically into our own ah-ha moments. We are SO blind when we are immature in our faith walk and it's amazing how we can justify our sin, until we suddenly see for ourselves that our lifestyle or behavior is grieving Him and how we are hurting ourselves with our choices. His ways are so much better. I don't know why we fight Him so long and so hard.

He is incredibly patient with us as we come to see for ourselves that everything He says is the truth. As we follow Him, spend time with Him in prayer and reading His precious love letter to us (the Bible), we start to understand the context of His laws and we gain such clearer appreciation for His heart for us. He isn't trying to make our life hard. When He gives us the test, He also provides the test key, and all the grace and wisdom to pass it. He literally couldn't make it any easier for us. He's not expecting us to be perfect so that He can wield some harsh judgment on us. Instead, He's showing us how impossible it is to be perfect and how He has made provision for that, which was extremely costly, and He just wants our heart. It's so beautiful.

We aren't giving up anything of value that this world has to offer by following Him. Instead, everything He gives us has such deeper value and meaning than we could have ever imagined. It's an incredibly generous exchange! When people are stubborn and resistant to Him, insisting they are their own God, it just makes me sad for them because they are so blind to what is available to them. They just simply don't get it.

This spiritual armor is very necessary because while we are on this earth, we have a spiritual enemy in Satan. He has a whole army of demonic leaders. I was so surprised to learn about how they have been assigned territory by Satan, and they each have a big army under them with one purpose…to kill, steal, and destroy the souls of people. They hunt us, like lions, looking for the vulnerable to devour. Here are some Bible verses on this subject:

"The thief comes only to steal and kill and destroy; I have come that they may have life and have it to the full". – John 10:10

"Be alert and of sober mind. Your enemy the devil prowls around like a roaring lion looking for someone to devour." 1 Peter 5:8

The enemy and his minions play dirty. They have rule over this earth, and they are much more powerful than we are, but NOT more powerful than Jesus Christ. His name holds ALL authority. As Christians, we have inherited His authority, so we can use His name to take power over the enemy. They shrink in fear of His name. We can't fight them, but we can wield His name and His word, standing firm while God's army fights them.

Our job is to stand and wield His power, understanding we have none without Him. This doesn't mean that we won't still experience attacks or bad circumstances, but it does mean that no weapon formed against us shall prosper, and it also means we have supernatural intervention in our circumstances. In other words, God's favor, spiritual protection, and the ability to do things we could never do on our own. There absolutely is a spiritual battle in our country, we're vulnerable when we are unarmed, so it's time we take up our spiritual armor!

Here's how I do it every morning before my feet hit the floor. I imagine myself putting on this armor working my way up from my feet, just like I'm putting on my physical clothes each day:

- **SHOES**: Father God, I put on my shoes of peace. Let peace follow me everywhere I go today and let me bring Your peace into every room and every conversation I engage in today.

- **BELT:** I put on my belt of truth. Please give me wisdom and discernment today in every circumstance and conversation.

- **BREASTPLATE**: I put on my breastplate of righteousness. If I am out of step with you in any way, please bring it to my attention so that I can be obedient and have no distance between us at all.

- **HELMET:** I put on my helmet of salvation. Thank you for what you did for me on that cross, Jesus. Because of You, I am of Your royal bloodline.

- **ROBE:** I put on my royal robe of favor. I am surrounded by Your uncommon favor, like a shield. (My husband and I have fun picking a robe color for the day.)

- **SHIELD:** I put on my shield of faith, holding it up above my head and quenching every dart the enemy sends. No weapon formed against me shall prosper. Get behind me, Satan, in the name of Jesus Christ. You have NO permission and NO power here today, over me or my children.

- **SWORD:** Father God, I put on my sword of Your word and wield that power today. You're the vine and I'm the branch. Apart from You, Lord, I can do nothing. But in you, and you in me, we will bear much fruit. (Scripture is the sword. His word is where the power is, not our words)

Then, I shift my focus to speaking to God's angels that are assigned to me. We each have them and they are here to help us.

- **GUARDIAN ANGELS**, I ask you to draw your divine swords of protection over my head and form a hedge of protection around me, my family, my children, grandchildren, home, friends, and my work. I ask for protection for our nation, our defenders, and our leaders. Let us all turn back to you God and please heal our land.

- **OPPORTUNITY ANGELS**, please go into the world today and stir up, bring about, cause to happen, and rain down on me and my family beautiful, abundant, prosperous, meaningful, fulfilling, fun, exciting, influential, and far-reaching blessings that line up with God's purpose for our lives. We dance in your spiritual sprinkler of blessings today like children delighting in you, Lord. In Jesus's name, Amen.

Chapter Seven

Pick Your Hard

I want to go ahead and warn you that what you'll learn on the following pages will be simple to understand, but it's not going to be EASY to do. The reason is because it will initially seem counterintuitive, and change is hard. But stay with me, please. It will be SO worth it in the end, as we now start diving into the deeper end of the pool.

Here are the 2 versions of HARD we are faced with in our country today:

HARD SCENARIO #1:

It's hard to become a helpless bystander as our country turns further away from God and our children and grandchildren lose their precious freedom.

HARD SCENARIO #2:

It's hard to discipline ourselves, yield to God, and adapt to new techniques to fight smarter for our children and grandchildren.

PICK YOUR HARD.

What's it going to be ladies? If you commit to HARD #2 with me, then here's a big virtual hug and let's roll up our sleeves together. We have work to do. Here we go!

Let's first take a quick snapshot of where we are, politically, in our country now. It's encouraging to see people leaving the Democratic Party. Many make statements like, *"I didn't leave my Party, my Party left me".*

Progressives have hi-jacked what's left of the Democrat Party and they have overplayed their hand. But although many people are fleeing this Party, it doesn't mean they are necessarily running to Republicans! We need to ask ourselves why that is!

I did a lot of research to try and uncover what it is about the Republican Party that people find so off-putting, especially minorities. I now see clearly that it has been a very successful campaign of exploiting emotions and hiding motivations through sympathetic messaging that has completely deceived people.

Did you know that the Republican Party was founded in 1854 for the main purpose of ending slavery? The Republicans are the Party of those 7 conservative values we talked about earlier, which encourage every American to take your potential out for a test drive and see what you can do. They respect people who are resourceful, who work and don't whine, who build character through hard work and who learn to adapt and overcome. It's the tough-love party, yes, but like that butterfly trying to break out of the cocoon, they understand the necessity of struggle and they embrace it.

There are numerous men and women who completely defy the narrative and rhetoric of the Democrat Party. Many chose not to participate in Affirmative Action because they wanted to achieve success based on their own effort and merit. So many amazing men and women that chose to believe in themselves found help all along the way, especially from white conservatives, when they put forth the effort. Names like Dr. Ben Carson, Dr. Carol Swain, Thomas Sewell, and others come to mind.

I must give the Democratic Party credit in the sense that they have been incredibly successful at perpetuating policies that award discrimination, advocate slavery, instigate Civil War, create horrible groups like the Ku Klux Klan, champion segregation, and promote public lynchings, all while claiming to be the friend of the minority and winning their unwavering loyalty. It's a serious feat they have pulled off.

Most of us are not educated on the intricacies of each Party, we just sort of hear the talking points on the news in the background of our lives and let emotion drive our opinion. That was certainly my story before entering this arena. I was SO oblivious to any details, I just voted for who I liked. I'm so embarrassed to admit that, but it's just the truth, and I am not alone. This is what each Party is counting on and what they drive their marketing strategy around. They know that people are busy, and they only absorb sound bites. I don't really see that changing anytime soon, which is why our conversations are so important within our personal sphere of influence.

So, when I researched and did my own polling on what Democrats think about Republicans, the point I just made was easily proven as it was all driven by emotion.

Here's what many of them think about Republicans:

- Republicans are the rich, country club Party.
- They are completely out of touch with the plight of the middle or lower class.
- They are harsh, hard-hearted, mean, and judgmental.

I was really shocked to read and hear this from people. How did we get here? Why do people think this about us? My first encounter with the Republican Party was performing for Ronald Reagan with my high school color guard in Atlanta. He captivated me when I heard him speak. I didn't find him to be any of those things listed above. He had such an impact on me that I voted Republican all my life.

Sidenote: I admit that I only voted in Presidential elections, and not all of them. Sometimes I'd forget to vote. I did not even know what a Primary election was, and I didn't follow any state or local races whatsoever. I was too busy in my own life to care about politics.

When I ran for Office and became entrenched in politics here in Tennessee, I was VERY disappointed in the behavior I saw in some Republicans. I saw some of those qualities that list portrays: hard-hearted, mean-spirited, harsh, judgmental, greedy, etc. I could also add a few. I saw that where the Democrats move in lockstep, the Republicans like independent silos. We certainly do have some elected Republicans who are what are referred to as RHINOs, which means Republican in Name Only. They run strong campaigns laced with lots of conservative promises, and then they change horses when they get to Washington, the State House, or their local elected Office. They play footsies with Democrats for mutual personal enrichment and sell out their constituents.

That kind of stuff is just going to happen in the trenches of politics. I won't ever excuse it, but I understand how it happens. Again, human nature never changes. But to prevent it, Republicans can become fierce watchdogs. They are very quick to eat their own if they deem it necessary. That's just an ugly part of politics, it goes on all the time in our Party because people are extremely passionate, in good and not so good ways.

The majority of the Republicans I've come to know have wonderful hearts, kind spirits, and a true sense of patriotism for our great country. But just like a few bad apples can spoil the whole bunch, there are some unsavory ones out there, too that give Republicans and Christians a bad name. I can see why some can turn people off so badly. We are certainly not winning Democrats or Independents to our Party by reinforcing their perception of us, even unknowingly.

I think a lot of what's driving bad behavior is anger and fear. Many Republicans are angry at how our country is being dismantled right before their eyes, so they are in war mode. They are also fearful that their children and grandchildren will inherit a land ruled by tyrants who will demand compliance or else; that freedom will be lost.

"Freedom is never more than one generation away from extinction. We didn't pass it to our children in the bloodstream. It must be fought for, protected, and handed on for them to do the same, or one day we will spend our sunset years telling our children and our children's children what it was once like in the United States where men were free." - Ronald Reagan's first Inaugural Address as Governor, 1967

It's never been easier for us to reach the Democrat Party because, as they have been emboldened to overplay their hand, many are seeing more clearly the hypocrisy of their Party for themselves and how much their terrible policies hurt people. Most Democrat voters have been well-conditioned by their Party to be driven by emotion. It's ironic to me that so many of them are super educated, can cite famous works, yet are so undiscerning of the context and so blinded by the emotion.

I've talked with a lot of Democrats over the last few years who ended up coming over to the Republican Party. They admit how they misconstrued facts, or were simply oblivious to them, and were driven purely by emotion. It happens repeatedly.

I have a great Podcast episode with a woman named Natalie Beisner. She lives in Los Angeles and was deeply entrenched in the world of theater there. She drove 100 miles to vote for Hillary Clinton and was a staunch pro-choice advocate. Natalie's conversion story to the Republican Party is really interesting and available on my Podcast channel or in the App.

Emotion and logic are like oil and water and the two simply don't mix. The more we try and spout logic into the faces of those driven by emotion, the more we will perpetuate division. We've got to find a better way.

What if we put ourselves in the shoes of those who are driven by emotion because they don't have a solid foundation? What if we gave them a safe place to let their guard down and gently guided them towards seeing the beauty of our values for themselves? Even Jesus welcomes us to the faith gently and starts us on "milk" as we then mature enough to handle "meat".

A lot of hardcore Republicans think that I'm out of my mind if we think we can win back our country gracefully. I used to have this one friend of mine, the hardcore type, call me regularly after he got my e-newsletter. For some reason he stayed on my mailing list, even though he didn't agree with my approach. We would get into some spirited debates.

I always understood where he was coming from. He believed it was going to take, in his words, "*an ass whooping*" to straighten this country out. I think there are a lot of people that could certainly benefit from one. Lord knows, I took my fair share of them in my life. But most Americans are just dazed and confused. That is something we can change.

If we don't adjust and intentionally set out to win this emotionally sensitive generation, we will lose our Republic. The beauty is that, underneath the emotion, they actually do agree with us so much more than they realize, we just have to help them to see it for themselves! This is where we learn to tap into our emotional intelligence. We need to be a soft place for them to land and the Oasis Party of hope. This is our moment to welcome people who are searching for Truth! This is our moment to WIN them to our great values!!!

Chapter Eight

Step #1 – Housekeeping

Women come hardwired with exceptional skills in emotional intelligence. This can be used for good or bad in our society; to seduce, to manipulate, to control others or to inspire, to connect, and to win consensus. But another gear kicks in when a woman becomes a mom. These exceptional skills of emotional intelligence now become SUPERPOWERS!

At this moment in our history, nobody is more qualified to influence an emotionally driven person or more motivated because our children are at stake. Just look at nature. When someone messes with a baby bear cub, and the mama bear is near, it doesn't end well. Her instincts kick in and you DON'T want to be on the receiving end of that. Moms are highly motivated to get in the cultural and political ring now because their babies are on the line. Most of them are going in with a LOT of passion, but they don't know "what" to do with it. Well, that ends today!

The first thing we must do is some internal housekeeping. I talked in the last chapter about how we need to be a soft place to land for someone who is lost and driven by emotion. We also must be a stable and safe place for them to feel comfortable in letting their guard down with us. If we are a hot mess, and an emotional basket case of our own, then I highly doubt if they will see us as safe, stable, or soft.

We also need to be sure we can check our own judgment at the door. The last way we want to come off is judgmental. God commands us to love our neighbors. That can be really hard to do when we share such opposing views. But again, remember, pick your hard! I have found that to achieve these 2 goals of being stable and being non-judgmental, it has to be authentic and not some act we are putting on for the conversation.

People can see right through it, and it won't win them. It will only further repel them. So, how do we make sure it's authentic? I think the quickest path to this is coming to terms with a few things in our own hearts.

Relationship

I heard Joyce Meyer say once that, "You can sit in a garage all day. That doesn't make you a car. You can sit in a church pew every Sunday. That doesn't make you a Christian."

Christianity is about relationship with Jesus. It's living our lives in a way that we "want" to please Him, and not grieve Him, because of everything he sacrificed for us. It's recognizing our own need for a Savior because we, as sinners, are incapable of keeping His Law and, without His grace, we would personally spend eternity separated from God.

One sin is not any worse than the other. Sin is Sin is Sin. Holy God hates lying as much as He hates adultery and as much as He hates murder. So, we must be careful not to compare our sin with others, EVEN THE OTHER POLITICAL PARTY, and put ourselves up on some righteous pedestal. He hates it all. We are all spiritual Lawbreakers, punishable by eternal separation from God. Let us NOT become "Modern Day Pharisees"!!!

Jesus came and took ALL our sins upon Himself. Out of incredible LOVE for us, He Who knew NO SIN became SIN. He was the ultimate and final sacrifice for our sins. He laid down His body and His life to BRIDGE that separation between God and us once and for all.

Because Jesus says, "*She's with me, Dad*", we are granted entry into God's Holy presence. We are sinless in God's eyes, thanks to the amazing GRACE (undeserved favor) of Jesus. NO other reason. He is THE WAY, THE TRUTH, and THE LIFE. NO ONE comes to The Father except through Jesus Christ. So, when people say to me, "*Diane, there MUST be more than one way to God.*" My answer is always the same. "*I'm just glad there is ONE because there didn't have to be, but there is ONLY ONE.*" Thank God Jesus loved us enough to make a way so that we would not live in eternal separation from Holy God.

We grow in maturity in our faith and God works within us to mold us more and more into the image of Christ, but NONE OF US HAVE ARRIVED! So, be humble in your conversations with others and remember that we are no better than anybody else when it comes to our salvation. Jesus loves them, too, just as much as He loves you.

Now, this doesn't mean that we "go along to get along". There are times when we must speak truth, but we do it in love. We pause in tough moments and ask God to give us the right words. We don't compromise our values whatsoever. But a harsh word or a judgmental tone is not the way to help open someone's eyes. The best thing that can happen for ANYONE is an encounter with Jesus. When they encounter you, let them see Him. YOU may be the only authentic Christian they have encountered. The Pharisees that ended up demanding Jesus' crucifixion were more concerned with being "seen" as righteous and maintaining their power, which resulted in their hard hearts. Don't Be a Modern-Day Pharisee!

We are all a work in progress and Jesus loves us all the same. So, let's check our judgment at the door. I do want to share one quick tip that really helps me. When I meet someone with an opposing view, I make an effort to notice the color of their eyes. This helps me to remember that God designed them and they are incredibly valuable to Him. I have an opportunity to win them to Him, yes, but more importantly I have an opportunity to demonstrate God's love for them.

Most people really believe they are on the right side of the issue. This is why it is called Amazing Grace. We once all believed that and by God's grace, though we were blind, now we see. Show grace and help others see.

Fruit of the Spirit

The fastest way to lose our influence with someone we are trying to win is to be caught being hypocritical. God told us we would know His followers by their fruit. Is ours still ripening, is it ready to eat, or is it rotten? Let's find out!

Love

I was amazed when I learned that I didn't have to "feel" like loving somebody to obey God's commandment to love them. Wait, what?!?! Love is more of an action than a feeling. We have so many different perceptions in our culture on what love means. It can be so confusing. This word has been completely manipulated and reworked to center around **feelings.** That could not be farther from God's definition of love. Feelings follow, I believe, but we don't lead with them to show love to others. *God tells us in the Bible that,*

> *"Love is patient, love is kind. It does not envy, it does not boast, it is not proud. It does not dishonor others, it is not self-seeking, it is not easily angered, it keeps no record of wrongs. Love does not delight in evil but rejoices with the truth. It always protects, always trusts, always hopes, always perseveres. Love never fails." -1 Corinthians 13:4-8*

I have found that my feelings can change on a dime, depending on the circumstance. God doesn't tell us that we won't "feel" anger, hurt, or any other emotion. Our job is to simply not "act" on them, but instead to walk in love. Here's a news alert: YOU CANNOT POSSIBLY DO THIS ON YOUR OWN!!! Here's the follow up: YOU DON'T HAVE TO!

This is why, after Jesus finished on earth and ascended to Heaven, that He sent us the Holy Spirit. His Spirit is with us, internally in our body as a temple, to guide us and help us with this every single day. The Spirit whispers His wisdom in our heart, prompts us gently, and helps restrain our tongue when we simply ask for His help. Many times, under my breath now a days, when I encounter a hostile person or someone wanting a fight, I'll say: "*God, give me the words*". He is SO faithful! Suddenly, I the ability to walk out that love requirement just kicks in. However, when I forget to ask Him and give into my emotions, it always ends poorly.

When you walk in love, you demonstrate obedience.

Joy

This can sound like such a "Churchy" word, I know, but I've come to better understand it and now I am so grateful for it! Joy doesn't mean the same thing as happiness.

Happiness is dependent on outside circumstances or people. Joy is ours, alone, with God. It's the secret sauce; that quiet contentment inside of just knowing He is with us and that He's got this. It's also a sense of security that no matter what comes or what happens, you're going to be okay because you're in His capable hands.

When you walk in joy, you demonstrate contentment.

Peace

I used to pray all the time for peace! But I've come to learn that I don't ever have to pray for peace again because I already have it. God gave it to us when he ascended to Heaven as one of His major parting gifts. Jeus said,

"Peace, I leave with you; my peace I give you. I do not give to you as the world gives. Do not let your hearts be troubled and do not be afraid." – John 14:27

We keep praying for it and He's already given it to us. We just need to tap into it by reminding ourselves we have it and thanking Him for it, and speaking this scripture out loud, as many times as necessary until it sinks in. We then find our rightful, peaceful place right in the eye of the storm. The storm can be raging all around you, but it does not have to be "in" you.

Consider being intentional about bringing peace WITH you into every room or conversation. Be the one that others can find peace in. Be like still waters that others are drawn to.

When you walk in peace, you demonstrate stability.

Patience

Lord, give me patience! How many times have we said that? I have discovered that the only way to get it is to develop it. There's really no other way. We need to decide to simply **wait well**. While we are waiting for our breakthrough, we can focus our minds on BEING exactly where we are, honoring ourselves through the pain or discomfort instead of trying to avoid it, keeping a good attitude while we wait it out. Changing the channel in our minds is one effective way we can do this. Friends can be a big help to add perspective.

I had a dear friend who said something so heartfelt to me that helped me so much. I shared with her how much I miss my son and how hard this distance between us is. She said,

"Diane, at least you know what it feels like to be a mother. That's a feeling I'll never know."
— She Shall Remain Anonymous

That stopped me in my tracks and showed me that even in our pain, while we're waiting for reconciliation with our children, we can be so grateful that we have been blessed to be mothers.

When you walk out patience, you demonstrate trust.

Kindness & Goodness

Jesus commanded us to go about doing good. We can smile and look for chances to drop sincere compliments. We can secretly pick up the tab of an elderly couple at a restaurant. We can choose to see others through God's eyes as His divine work of art, understanding that we are ALL a work in progress. When we stop looking at people through the lens of how they make us feel and instead, consider how much God must love them, then it becomes easier to be kind. It's not contrived, but it is sincere.

When you walk in kindness and goodness,
you demonstrate grace.

Faithfulness

This is a commitment to God that we wholeheartedly offer and that we choose to display to the world. I like to call it a yielding to Him. We gladly give Him our heart, our decisions, our struggles, our pain, and our desires. He is so faithful to us in showing us we can trust Him with all these things.

It's like a marriage in the sense that we are in a committed relationship with Him, and we don't stray from it with outside temptations or distractions. We keep ourselves focused on Him and stay close to Him in spiritual intimacy.

When you walk out faithfulness, you demonstrate loyalty.

Gentleness

This is a humility that radiates from us in knowing that all our talent, ability, knowledge, strength, and blessings come from God. There is nothing we can take credit for. He created us and

He has predestined a purpose for our lives. We are so grateful, and that gratitude spills out of us so that we can then pour out onto others from a full cup, not a depleted one.

When you walk in gentleness, you demonstrate humility.

Self-control

I love to watch movies that portray characters who display an incredible ability to remain calm, cool, and collected, while everyone else is in total freakout mode. I aspire to that. To be able to think clearly while everyone else is panicking or immovable by someone determined to provoke you, is an incredible mastery of emotions. We don't have to be slave to our emotions. I can hear some of you, right now, saying, "*Diane, I can't help it. Whatever I think is just going to come right out of my mouth.*" Maybe you see that as just being honest and not letting things bottle up inside. I get that, but I'm here to tell you, it's not in alignment with what God teaches. There are way too many scriptures that tell us to be slow to anger, to bridle our tongue, etc. That attitude is how meltdowns happen and I've already shown how those don't end well. God calls us to a higher standard of behavior and that's where the real power is!

When you walk out self-control you display discipline.

Spring Cleaning

This would be a time to do a major spring cleaning in our lives. Maybe it means cleaning your social media stream of mean-spirited or snarky posts that can be seen as hypocritical. Resisting the urge to "like" or "laugh" at mean-spirited Social Media posts or verbal comments from others.

Be mindful of the fact that we live in a fishbowl as Christians. Our children, family, and friends are always watching. Become much more intentional about spending time with God in prayer, opening your Bible, and quietly listening for His voice in your heart because we need His help. In order to successfully tap into the "PEACE THAT SURPASSES UNDERSTANDING" and walk out the Fruit of The Spirit throughout the day, we need His gentle reminders to turn to Him. Listen for His reminders and choose not to be a slave to our emotions.

And, hey, if you blow it like I did, admit it. Own it. Choke down that big slice of humble pie and apologize immediately. Don't try to justify it or brush it off. It'll be hard initially, but when we admit our mistakes and frailties, God can step in and do great things to repair it.

Releasing Offense

Our last bit of housekeeping to do is to become immune to offense if we hope to influence at the highest level. When we truly know WHOSE we are, that we are of Royal Blood, then it becomes an unshakeable identity.

I saw a Facebook post recently that showed a picture of a lamb and a poisonous snake. That lamb was unaffected by the presence of the snake because it is immune to its bite. Apparently, snake venom antibodies are made from lamb's blood, which I find VERY neat!!! Evidence of God is everywhere.

We give away our power when we allow mean-spirited words to hurt us. We can decide ahead of time how to handle mean-spirited attacks. First, remember that these are NEVER of God! When our character is attacked, the brain's natural reaction is to DEFEND ourselves or that belief. Stop and think for a minute about the thoughts that go through your head later after you've been offended:

- *"How could they even think such an awful thing about me? Is that how people see me?"*
- *"What a horrible thing to say...do other people say those things behind my back?"*
- *"Is it true? Am I really like that?"*

Now think about it for a minute...In each of these scenarios, we are giving someone else a LOT of power over us when we choose to be offended. We're basically knee-jerk reacting and allowing their words or actions to take priority over what Jesus says about us. Whose opinion matters more to you? The offender's opinion or Jesus' opinion?

Instead, we can adopt the following internal dialogue, and spiritually mature attitude, which deprives others of their power to offend us. (This internal dialogue is **not** meant to be said out loud.)

- *"We're all a work in progress. God knows where I've been. I haven't arrived. I'll be growing and learning until I die. So, God's opinion of me, and His correction where necessary, is what matters."*

- *"Those hurtful words don't line up with what God says about me. God's nature is not mean-spirited. If there is something that needs to be addressed, He will work it out in me. But this is not His character."*

- *"We all have our blind spots. Blindness in others only stokes my compassion for them, rather than infuriating me. The best thing that could happen would be for them to SEE the truth in this situation, so I'm going to pray for that."*

When we KNOW WHOSE WE ARE and we choose to live for that audience of ONE, it shows up in our facial expressions, our tone of voice, and the RESPONSE we choose. It also totally protects us from the trap of offense. It's such a mature way of approaching the challenges we face with people. We stop handing over our power to people who would only hurt us with it.

That is EXACTLY what they are trying to do...to hurt you. Don't give them that power. Take the "teeth" out of their comments. YOU have the power to do that! And keep in mind that it doesn't matter AT ALL if they appreciate it or receive it or not. It doesn't even matter if it's a member of your family. I know family can often offend or hurt us the most. Responding rather than reacting is even more effective with family. Gently excusing yourself from the conversation, in a loving way, is the epitome of self-control.

You're not living for their approval...you're living for an audience of ONE! Be different. Be intriguing to people. Be a "trout" who is discerning, rather than a "catfish" who will just bite at anything. It takes an extra level of spiritual maturity and self-control to "respond" instead of "knee-jerk react"! That's a VERY powerful place to influence from. When we are grounded about Whose we are, we don't allow offense to get on the inside of us. You become VERY powerful and a serious threat to the enemy when you know WHOSE you are, and that offense just doesn't even phase you.

Don't give into that temptation to be offended...that just screams: AMATEUR! Knee-Jerk reactions in a heated moment of offense don't take any discipline or thought whatsoever. We simply blurt out our words to defend ourselves or defend our position. I like to equate this thought to making an exchange at the Macy's counter. Offense doesn't fit us anymore, so we're exchanging offense for something that fits us much better...influence.

We can even learn to become tickled by it. This gives us, the wherewithal to step back, take a breath, and ask God to give us the words in that heated moment. We become immovable to hairpin triggers. We realize they are just an enemy tactic, we become wise to it, and we remember we have the Lamb's immunity.

Later, in our quiet prayer time with God, we are always asking Him to reveal truths to us about ourselves. We can ask Him if there is something He wants us to learn or see from that experience. But we become wiser as we do this to not fall prey to enemy tactics. It also helps us develop compassion for those who offend us when we learn to change the questions in our head.

- *How did this person get so lost?*
- *This is a human being that God loves just as much. I may be the only Jesus they encounter. How do I want to represent Him?*

We can refuse to give someone the power to hurt us. So, choose ahead of time, your response so that you don't react. Become seasoned and highly skilled on the battleground.

God tells us in the Bible,

"Good sense and discretion make a man slow to anger, and it is his honor and glory to overlook a transgression or an offense without seeking revenge and harboring resentment."

- Proverbs 19:11

Chapter Nine

Step #2 – Entertaining

O ne of the things we can do better as Republicans is learn to entertain someone else's worldview. NOW WAIT!!! I am NOT saying we have to further "mediate" or "compromise". We have done enough of that, no doubt! We can't compromise our values for anyone! But we will never be able to win people to our values if we haven't first earned permission to be heard. Now, let me preface this chapter by saying this step is NOT intended for the radical left! This is for more moderate people who usually vote Democrat because their family always did, or Independent because they can't stomach Republicans. It could also be for people who don't typically vote at all, especially younger people.

Earning Permission to Be Heard

It's very difficult to influence total strangers because we don't have any trust equity built. We have a much better chance of influencing people who know, like, and trust us. That trust should never be weaponized. We MUST come from a genuine place. But opportunities for common ground to bubble up to the surface can happen naturally when we set the atmosphere for entertaining and resist the temptation to prove we're right.

One of our first steps in entertaining is to become a curious listener. Maya Angelou said, "*Nobody cares what you know until they know how much you care.*" We need to be willing to open our minds and entertain how other people view the world. And don't be concerned that you will be swayed because you won't when you are rooted in truth. But you just might learn something valuable about this person, allowing them to open up safely, and it just may reveal some common ground between you. When we listen with curiosity and we make a genuine attempt to connect with someone, then they drop their guard. But if your motive is to "convert them", they will sense it and your attempt will fail. It's also just a crummy way to approach people.

How many times have we lost respect for someone who pretends to be our friend only to later find out they wanted something from us and were just buttering us up? I hate that. I'm sure you do, too. And we feel a sense of betrayal when we become aware of it. **Don't be that person!**

PLEASE understand that our role in this ENTERTAINING step is to simply focus on the actual person, the experiences they've been through that helped shape their view of the world, and WHY. That's it. Nothing more. Once they relax around you and feel you are not going to judge or force your opinion, you will have earned permission to be heard and they will more likely want to hear what you have to say next.

Don't listen to manipulate! Simply listen to understand! The scenario here is that you're talking with someone who has expressed a viewpoint that you don't agree with.

In this step, you will:

- Reserve judgment.
- Reserve your opinion.
- Reserve your response.

Instead, you're just a curious listener. You're leaning in and making curious conversational starters that look something like this:

99

- *"I really want to see this through your eyes…help me understand where you're coming from."*
- *"Wow, that's really interesting…tell me more about how you came to that conclusion."*

Remember, you're just trying to understand! Not speak!!! The more you genuinely listen and care to understand, the more trust will be built. Their stories may remind you of a story of a friend you had or something similar you've experienced. You're trying to uncover common ground.

WARNING, Will Robinson: If this does trigger a memory or experience for you, resist the temptation to go too far down a rabbit trail of giving them all the details of YOUR experience. Instead, just acknowledge that you understand and say, *"I've been through something similar."* Maybe give a detail or two here but, unless they ask you to tell them more, keep the focus on them.

If they start to take you down a long rabbit trail that you don't want to go down, you can control the flow of the conversation by redirecting questions back towards something else you want to know about them. People love to talk about themselves, so when you change the subject, but it's still about them, you're okay. We can love people through their blindness. Jesus loved us through a lot more than that and even loved the very guards nailing Him to the Roman cross. So, I think we can handle this!

Echo Chambers Are Fun, But Useless

The better we understand the viewpoints of other people, the better influencers we become. We must get out of our echo chamber and become curious listeners! This is a crucial step in our ability to influence! Plus, again, you just might learn something useful. Let's get out of our tent!

Being around like-minded people is natural and gives us confidence to go out and take a stand in the world. But commiserating is not helpful. Take that to God instead. Become genuinely interested in seeing life from someone else's perspective.

I like to watch other news stations to better understand how they are getting into the hearts and minds of others; to see how they are seducing them with their messaging? A TV show that has helped me understand their side of issues and taught me a lot about the political process is *The Circus*. I binge watched it on Showtime and Paramount+. It has been SO helpful to get inside the psyche a bit of the "left". It's painful to watch, at times, but it is very eye-opening.

Another thing you can do is take people you know who have opposing views to lunch and listen to where they're coming from. It gives you such a depth of understanding behind these policies and narratives. Compassion can pour out of us when we hear about how they arrived at their conclusions. It softens our hearts towards them. I took a woman to lunch who had relocated to Tennessee from California. She was a progressive Democrat, and we couldn't have been further apart on our ideology.

I applied the techniques I'm showing you and our time together was so sweet. I understood her a lot better and her reasons behind her beliefs, even if I didn't agree. Her parting words were, *"This is the best conversation I have ever had with a Republican."* And then she hugged me and told me I had *"given her a lot to think about"*. THAT'S the statement we are looking for!!! It is the absolute best we can hope for, y'all. That's what success in a conversation looks like. God does the rest.

Discernment is being able to distinguish what is important in a conversation and, more importantly, what is NOT important. It is the ability to know when to speak, but more importantly, to know when to HUSH. I really believe discernment is a huge part of wisdom. Discernment is a GIFT from GOD! People can tell when you're trying too hard or when you're conjuring up your next statement without listening to them. The Holy Spirit will bring things to our remembrance at exactly the right time...don't worry that we're going to forget what we want to say. It's much more important to let someone know they have been heard than to make your point.

For some reason, we women hate silence in a conversation. We find it awkward, and we try to fill it up with something, anything! Silence won't bite, ladies. It's okay to let a moment linger. But conversations are much more than just what is being said. It's about the nuances. It's sifting through what is real and what is not. It's picking up on what's not being said just as much as what is being said. Pray for God to give you that wisdom! When people really feel that you are willing to hear them, it goes a LONG way in earning permission to be heard!

In your own mind, be rolling questions like these around:

- *What's the MOST helpful thing that could happen in this conversation?*
- *How can I best serve this person in this moment?*
- *What does this person wish that I could understand about them?*

Is my opinion on this matter really necessary to say out loud, or can I let it go this time? The Bible explains to us that wisdom is more precious than gold or silver, that it is the foundation for happiness, and that God pours it out to us freely if we ask Him for it. Here are a few of my favorite scriptures on this subject:

"Even fools are thought wise if they keep silent, and discerning if they hold their tongues."

-Proverbs 17:28

"Be wise in the way you act toward outsiders; make the most of every opportunity. Let your conversation be always full of grace, seasoned with salt, so that you may know how to answer everyone." -Colossians 4:5-6

"If any of you lacks wisdom, you should ask God, who gives generously to all without finding fault, and it will be given to you."

-James 1:5

Chapter Ten

Step #3 - Gardening

*P*atience is the key to gardening!!! It takes time and faithful steps, like planting, watering, and nurturing before anything blooms! There is NOTHING we can do or say that will make another human being bloom faster. Steps can't be skipped and only God knows which stage of the process they are in. He knows the secret places of someone's soul. Only HE knows where they've been, why they believe the way they do, and HOW to reach them. Transformation is internal and there is just nothing we can do about that.

When a seed is planted in the ground, the shell slowly disintegrates as the life inside of it eventually emerges. The transformation of someone's heart and mind is the same way. It takes place internally and in darker, more secret places. It could be a sudden epiphany in someone's darkest midnight hour. It could be in a sad moment of grief that a long-awaited truth is revealed. It could be a dream in the wee hours of the morning that wakes someone up with a sudden rush of clarity. The point is that it takes place internally and often in dark places.

The good news is that our only job is to SOW SEEDS. That's it. Our words carry a great deal of weight. Make sure yours are laced with grace and a desire to see someone step into the life that is waiting for them. Both life and death are in the tongue. Choose to plant seeds of Life into others.

Each time we see them, we water that seed a little more, and other people God brings across their path will also do some watering. Only God knows how many waterings it will take before they bloom. Let's face it, for some of us, it takes a while. Sin is fun. There's a lot of seemingly cool things the world has to offer, and we don't like party poopers.

But, as the seeds are being watered in someone's life, God is working on their heart. What happened for me, over a long period of time, is the stuff that once seemed fun wasn't fun anymore. It wasn't because I felt like someone took it away from me, I just simply didn't WANT those things in my life anymore. I was tired of feeling like I always needed a vacation from my stressful life. I was tired of feeling empty inside and unfulfilled. I grew weary of people who drained my energy and took advantage of me. I realized that I was being used and not truly loved.

Those seasons of watering are invaluable to me now. God knows how to do it at a pace we can handle and in a way that we draw closer to Him, as we realize He is the real place we find fulfillment, refreshment, and love. There is nothing this world can give us that fulfills us for more than an hour or so. When we understand the magnitude of what is available to us in God's way of living, our *want to* simply changes.

Have you ever met someone who just doesn't feel like drinking or smoking anymore? Like they just lost the craving for it? That's kind of what it's like for those we are trying to influence. They will eventually just lose their taste for the things of this world and realize for themselves that God has been waiting on them. It's a beautiful thing.

We can see now how amateur efforts, such as aggressively belaboring our point, are a complete waste of time. Think about YOUR own life where you had a major epiphany. Was it internal? I'm guessing yes!

Releasing The Outcome

We are NOT Jesus Jr.! God does not expect us to change another person. He knows we are not capable of that. Only God knows another person's heart and even He doesn't force outcomes. He makes the offer like a gentleman and people have free will to either accept it or not.

So, why do we put so much pressure on ourselves to change or convert people? Some people just want to be right, but I think for most of us, it's because we care so much. Although that is admirable, it's also futile. We need to STOP IT, IMMEDIATELY! The pressure, that is, not the caring.

When we release the outcome, it also purifies our motive! This is huge!!! It changes the atmosphere from pressure to peace. When we release the outcome and understand our role in influencing, then it takes all the pressure off us, AND the conversation!

People will be so much more receptive when they don't feel that pressure coming from us. They aren't tensing up…instead they are opening up and we have an opportunity to plant that seed just a little deeper into their spirit. The quality of the planting and ability to take root is dependent on how we plant it.

Remember when I was telling you about my rifle Coach, Richard, earlier? Well, 30 years later, we reconnected on Facebook. He came to one of my *Nashville Unleashed* shows in Atlanta. We always ended our shows with Amazing Grace. He loved it and was raving about how he was watching the impact it had on the audience. After the show, he shared something that has stuck with me now for years.

He said, "*Your job is to sow! The harvest is none of your business. Don't focus on how many seeds are in the apple, but on how many apples can come from that one seed.*" In other words, concentrate on the quality of the seed I am planting and don't worry about the outcome. The outcome is God's business. Richard has been a tremendous mentor in my life in many ways and I'm so grateful for him.

Most people are extremely attached to their beliefs, especially when there is a lot of peer support, and they are not quick to entertain new ideas or opposing ideas. It's almost like a defense mechanism within us to protect our belief system. We all have it, no matter which side of the aisle we are on. When we are asked a question, our brains immediately either go to work on trying to answer it or rejecting it because it threatens our belief system.

The question then becomes how can we shorten that runway? How can we shorten the time between them hearing the truth and them accepting the truth? I truly believe it is in our presentation of that truth.

When we ask a question, we must do it in such a way that we appeal to their belief system, not try and force them to disrupt or abandon their belief system. This is what I mean by strategic. The question must tap into the things/ideas that they already care about and gently introduce another option in the belief system they already carry. In other words, it must become an extension of their belief system, almost like an evolution of it, rather than a departure from it.

People like to arrive at their own conclusions. They resist being coerced into a new conclusion.

Lingering Questions are the most powerful seeds we can plant in the hearts and minds of people with opposing views.

The ingredients of a lingering question are:

1. **They are compassionately crafted**. We demonstrate our empathy as we explore opposing ideas with people, rather than coming in with iron fists.

2. **They are responsive, not reactionary**. Knee-jerk reactions are not helpful. A cool head and intentional response garners respect, even if it is never admitted.

3. **They stop someone in their tracks**. They're stunned because they have never quite thought about it like that. They don't have an immediate answer, so it gives you an advantage to gently exit the conversation during this silence. More on that in a moment.

4. **They linger in the person's heart and mind long after the conversation ends.** They can't get it out of their head. The question haunts them until they see you again.

5. **They invite further discussion**. Rather than avoiding you the next time they see you or gearing up for a fight, they are anxious to talk to you again.

These questions are designed in a way to not fight against their belief system, but to add layers to it for them to consider and arrive at their own conclusion...their own "ah ha" moment.

As they work through their own belief system and consider the things they already care about and build on those concepts, THE TRUTH will be revealed to them, and they have the best chance of seeing for themselves that they have been deceived. When you are a safe one for them to admit that to, rather than waiting with a big "I told you so" or making them feel stupid that they had been so deceived, you can win their friendship as well as a vote for conservative values. So, we need to make a crucial decision today: Do we want to be right, or do we want to win people?

A powerful question that lingers in a person's mind, instead of a threat to their belief system, is a powerful path to turning our country around, one heart at a time, at scale. Think of yourself as a modern-day Yoda, only waaaay prettier!

Chapter Eleven

Lingering Questions Catalog

Lingering questions are what we use to guide people to their own **"Ah-Ha Moment"**. They are the powerful **"seeds"** we plant in the **"Gardening"** step of our training. This Catalog is meant to give you a conversational starting point on various tough topics. Think of it like training wheels until you learn to ride the bike. You MUST practice and role play in a safe setting with people you trust. The more you hear yourself do this and speak these questions, the more likely you'll be to do this in real life!

You'll get better and better at this the more you do it and it'll give you confidence to craft YOUR OWN questions and come up with them in the moment. It's neat how this becomes more natural the more you do it.

As we approach these uncomfortable conversations, here are a few things to keep in mind when you deliver a lingering question:

- Our body language should be assertive, but never aggressive.
- We want to speak compassionately and with a tone of certainty, but not superiority!
- We want to be succinct, straight to the point. Don't dilly-dally around or go on and on trying to get to the question.

Once you drop the question, you MUST make an excuse to gently exit the room. I cannot express this strongly enough! The reason is because this will likely shock them, or silence them, and you don't want to dilute the impact of that question. It's important that it's the last thing they hear in conversation with you as you kindly bid them farewell.

The idea is that this seed will have every opportunity to take root and then when they see you again, you have a new opportunity to water it. They won't be running from you next time because you came on too strong, either. They will actually want to talk to you. At that point, you can drop your next question on them, leave the conversation, rinse, and repeat.

After a few of these encounters, you will have made a significant impact, and you may even win them. So, let's look at how they work in conversation with someone you're trying to influence.

When discussing the issue of abortion, you'll hear many arguments for a pro-choice stance:

- A woman has a right to choose what happens with her own body.

- A woman shouldn't be forced to become a mom before she's ready.

- It's a fetus, not a child, until it is viable and can survive outside the womb.

- You are pro-birth, not pro-life, because you never address how that mother is supposed to care for that child after it's born.

- There are already so many kids in foster care, why would you want to add to that?

There are other arguments that are nothing short of evil, but we're just going to discuss the ones you're most likely to run into with the average person you're trying to influence. Again, keep in mind, this book is not meant to be applied to highly radical people.

Although we know that a child is viable upon conception, that its precious little heartbeat signifies life, that God knits us together in our mother's womb, and that every life has a divine purpose, for people who don't know God yet, these truths don't often resonate with them right away.

Something I found so interesting when I was studying this during my campaign is that only 6% of abortions result from rape and incest. I know that number is likely higher, since many rapes are not reported, but even if you tripled the number, that would still mean that 82% of abortions are elective based mostly on convenience. That just breaks my heart. But in a culture that oversexualizes everything, and tries to convince women that their sexuality is where their power is, what do we expect?

I understand the mentality. When I was younger and in the music industry, I was encouraged to wear sexy clothing, attract men, and I embraced that. I loved the attention, and it does feel empowering to be able to command a room with your sexual energy, but the feeling is so fleeting. It's the wrong kind of attention. It has no substance whatsoever. I found that out the hard way. Nothing could be less empowering. Having lived both lifestyles, and been very promiscuous early in my life, I can tell you that God's design for marriage and motherhood is the most empowering feeling in the world.

So, how do we handle these common arguments without getting into a huge shouting match?

Lingering Questions on Abortion:

- Help me because I really am trying to understand. **Here's where I get lost**...It's heartbreaking how slaves were counted as only 3/4 of a person by government or how millions of Jewish men, women, and children were marched into gas chambers and extinguished because a government considered them disposable. I know we're not going to agree on this today, but let me leave you with this question: **Who determines the value of another human being, if not God?** Just some food for thought. Great seeing you today! I've gotta run, but let's talk again when I see you next week.

- I am really trying to understand where you're coming from, and I know we are not going to see eye to eye on this today. But I want to keep trying. Help me with this...What's the first thing a paramedic checks for at the scene of an accident? Yes, a pulse. What does it signify? Yes, Life. So, **if a heartbeat always indicates life at the scene of an accident, why wouldn't it signify life in the womb?**

I'm so sorry, I've gotta run, but maybe we can talk about it more when I see you again. Have a great day!

- Thanks for sharing and I really am trying to see things from your point of view. Maybe you can help me understand this...in a courtroom, a convicted felon suffers 2 sentences for taking the life of a pregnant woman. **How can it be wrong, and even punishable, to kill an unborn child in a courtroom yet not be wrong in the court of public opinion?** Just something to ponder. Good seeing you today. I've gotta run, but I'll look forward to picking up where we left off.

- You seem very solid in your stand on this issue, and I respect your right to that stand. You remind me a lot of Abby Johnson. There's a movie about her called Unplanned. She was a strong advocate for abortion, she had an abortion herself, and she was one of Planned Parenthood's top employees...until...her clinic was short-staffed one day and she was asked to assist with the abortion procedure. She was watching the ultrasound monitor and saw the fetus fighting for its life against the instruments. It changed EVERYTHING for her, and now she is one of the strongest Pro-Life advocates out there. So, my question to you would be: **If you knew had to watch a child fighting for its life inside the womb, do**

you think it would change your mind about abortion like it changed Abby's? Don't answer me now. Maybe catch her movie and see what you think. I'm so sorry I've gotta run. Great to see you and I look forward to seeing ya next week.

- I believe I see your point. You're not denying that the fetus is a life, you just still feel that the woman should have a right to extinguish that life if she chooses. Okay, so here's where I get lost...If you were to overhear a child being beaten and crying for help in a neighboring house, the neighbor could argue, "This is my house and none of your business." But the cops would override them to protect the life of that child. So, my question to you today is: **Isn't a child just as defenseless, whether in a structural or biological home?** It's worth pondering. So sorry I've gotta run! Let's continue our discussion next time I see you. I always welcome that with you.

Let's shift now to CRT (Critical Race Theory) and DEI (Diversity, Equity, and Inclusion). CRT hides under many different names in schools. This is a way to fool parents into thinking it isn't being taught, especially in states who have banned it. Some of the names it hides behind are *Wit & Wisdom, Culturally Responsive Teaching, the 1619 Project, Affinity Groups, Anti-Racism Training, Reconstructing Curriculum,* and a host of other names.

This ideology basically teaches kids that they are either an oppressor or they are oppressed, based on their skin color, because racism is baked into our culture. DEI is basically the same thing, only it shows up in the workplace and in organizations rather than schools.

We covered earlier how America is built on meritocracy, meaning that we work for and earn the things that we achieve. But Affirmative Action was put in place after the Civil Rights Act of 1964, and basically required decision makers to meet quotas of a certain number of minorities on their payroll, on their boards, in college admissions, etc. whether they were qualified or not.

The idea of it seemed well-intentioned and was supposed to enforce the Civil Rights Act, but it ended up being reverse discrimination and was struck down in 2023 by the Supreme Court for violating the Equal Protection Clause of the 14th Amendment. DEI is sure to follow this path. People should rise or fall based on their effort, not their race. There is nothing blocking hard-working people from achieving anything they are willing to work for.

Lingering Questions on Racism & CRT

- I'm really trying to understand where you're coming from. Here's where I get lost: **Doesn't seeing ourselves as victims make us our own oppressors?** Just some food for thought. It's great to see you, as always. See ya soon.

- I can see that you sincerely believe CRT is not being taught in schools and I would love to believe that, too. Here is where I get lost...an entire generation of children have emerged with the notion that the system is rigged against people of color, that black people are oppressed, and that white people are their privileged oppressors. It's like they all got the same memo across the country. So, my question to you would be: **If that memo didn't come out of the public schools, where did it come from?** I'd love to discuss this further when I see you next. I'm sorry, I've gotta run. Great seeing you today!

- There's a lot to unpack here and I know these conversations aren't easy. Here's where I get lost...We are so inspired by the numerous rags to riches stories, of all races and ethnicities, because it celebrates how the human spirit can overcome. **So, my question for you is does CRT inspire anyone?** Just something to ponder. I've gotta run. See ya next week.

- Slavery has been a tragic part of history in every country in the world for centuries, and America has that stain on our history, too. Here's where I get lost. As a person, most of us have extremely regretful parts of our past we would love to undo. **If repentance and forgiveness are the spiritual path to healing, could it also be the path for the healing of America?** Just something to consider. I've gotta run, but I'd love to talk more about this when I see you again.

Now let's look at the LGBTQ+ community and especially the Trans movement, which is heart wrenching. So many of our children are having suggestions planted in their young minds about their sexuality, and then with the stroke of a pen from a therapist or doctor, they can be on an operating table undergoing mutilation of their young bodies and parents can do nothing to stop it. I've never seen anything so cruel in my entire life, apart from abortion.

The irony is that this is sold to today's young people as a form of compassion. They find very compassionate sounding name for it, such as gender affirming; to affirm their "true identity". We know that our identity is in Christ alone and He does not make gender mistakes, especially at this alarming rate, but they don't know that. This is more confusion tactics from the enemy targeted at our vulnerable children and it is dark. Young people today are starving for identity and purpose, and they find solace in these seemingly "inclusive" communities. I explained earlier how we, unknowingly, created this spiritual void in the hearts of our children with our faith being backburned in our homes and lives. So, if these precious children later come to know Christ and understand their true identity, horror sets in when they wake up to the deception they have been under. Unfortunately, they've made permanent changes to their bodies that are irreversible.

It is all part of the spiritual warfare we discussed earlier. The nearest and dearest to God's heart are our children. There is an innocence and purity children have in God's eyes. He references it many times in scripture. But the enemy comes to kill, steal, and destroy. How better to get back at God than to destroy His most precious creation?

We MUST learn how to gently wake up our children about this. So many doctors will tell families that if they don't go along with the child's decision to change genders, then the children will commit suicide. What an awful position for any parent. Guiding our precious children to understand their identity in Christ is the way we love our children best. I do want to recommend two people to you that have helped me a LOT to understand the LGBTQ community and debunk a lot of their arguments.

Becket Cook lived the gay lifestyle for 20 years in Los Angeles, in full regalia. He found Christ and turned his life completely around and now has a Podcast to help us all understand it better, as well as how to love gay people to the Lord.

Rosaria Butterfield was a VERY devout political gay activist in her early career. She was a Professor at Columbia, living a lesbian lifestyle, a strong feminist fighting "patriarchy", felt she was doing all the right things by helping feed the poor and bringing relief to the underprivileged and those suffering. She had an encounter with Jesus and has now been a Pastor's wife for 20 years. Her testimony is extraordinary and will give you some wonderful insight into the deception of the gay and trans lifestyle.

Lingering Questions on Transgenderism

- I appreciate your insights into this because I genuinely want to understand. **Where I get lost is if gender can be fluid, how does it make sense to make permanent and irreversible changes to a person's body?** I've gotta run, but I would love to pick this conversation up where we leave off when I see ya next week.

- I appreciate your insights into this because I genuinely want to understand. Here's where I get lost. With more social acceptance around gender identity confusion and more support for the LGBTQ community than ever before, I find it so sad that suicide rates are only rising and so are videos of regret after gender reassignment surgery. **So, my question is why do you think these numbers are going in the unexpected direction?** Let's discuss this more when I see you next week. Gotta run. Bye for now.

- I appreciate your insights into this because I genuinely want to understand. Where I get lost is that for centuries, Doctors did all the diagnosing. They arrived at their diagnosis after testing, examination, research, and deductions. They have malpractice insurance in case they make mistakes. Now children are diagnosing themselves and demanding Doctors perform life-altering operations. My question would be: **What is the remedy if a child misdiagnoses themselves?** Just some food for thought and maybe we can discuss this more when I see you next week. Gotta run.

- Thank you for your insights into this because I really do want to understand. Where I get lost is how a sacred oath

Doctors take is to "Do No Harm". So, my question I'd like to leave us with today is: **How is "harm" to be measured...is it measured based on fluid emotional distress or permanent physical regret?** Just some food for thought. I've gotta run, but I look forward to seeing you tomorrow and maybe we can pick up where we left off. Bye for now.

- Thank you for your insights into this because I really do want to understand. **Help me understand how gender can be a social construct, yet that someone can be trapped in the wrong body.** It's worth pondering and a discussion I'd love to finish with you when I see ya next week. For now, I've gotta run...see ya next week!

- I'm genuinely trying to understand, so please be patient with me. **If genitals don't define a person's sex, how does removing them affirm it?** I'm going to have to wrap my head around that one. Great to see you and let's pick this up in our next discussion.

We have an entire catalog of Lingering Questions in the Lady Up America APP where we cover **many more hot topics**. I invite you to download the APP and join our community because we are updating this catalog all the time and practicing together.

Chapter Twelve

Parting Prayer

G od tells us in the Bible in 2 Chronicles 7:14, "If my people, which are called by my name, shall humble themselves, pray and seek my face and turn from their wicked ways, then I will hear from heaven, and will heal their land." That's a tall order from the Lord, but one I know many of us moms believe with all our hearts. We are motivated to leave our children and grandchildren the same freedoms we have enjoyed. The steps you've learned in this book give us the right tools as we cope with our anger and fear over the trajectory of our country.

Remember that politics is always downstream of culture. If we can change the culture, we can change the political landscape, but the culture changes must happen first. My vision is that if Christian moms can master the steps in this book and apply them to their everyday conversations, at scale, we can change the culture!

This is where the power truly is, not in government. Moms have superpowers of influence in our culture. People don't listen to politicians; they listen to each other! My hope for you is that you are so inspired by what you have learned here today that you step fully into your own power and that it is contagious with all the women you know. I hope you will help me train them up so that we can turn out an army of incredible moms to win hearts and minds on the toughest spiritual battleground of our lifetime.

We will not win everybody, just like Jesus and the Disciples showed us. But we can win many. It brings to mind the story of the starfish on the beach. A woman walked along the beach and saw hundreds of starfish that had washed up on shore and were dying. She was doing her best to reach as many of them as possible and throw them back into the ocean before they died. A man yelled to her and said, "This is futile, so many of them are going to die, so why does it matter?" As she picked up the next one and threw it into the ocean, she said, "It sure matters to this one." That is the spirit in which we have to approach this. Let's reach the ones we can.

My prayer for you: *Father God, please bless this precious woman and her family. Please give her confidence and the ability to walk in the peace You have left for her as she steps into her spiritual power of winning hearts and minds to you. Help her to feel your favor in every conversation she attempts and give her Your words. Let those words take root in the hearts of the people she encounters and please use her to let this lost generation know how much You love them. Please help her efforts to be fruitful and to contribute to turning our nation back to You so that You will heal our land. I pray this in Jesus's name. Amen*

I would love to hear your success stories as you take these techniques into the world! Please stay in touch with me, sweet sister in Christ.

 10%OF ALL BOOK & APP SALES DONATED TO PREGNANCY CARE CENTER TN

Download the Lady Up America APP in your Google or Apple store now to go deeper into these concepts. It is the Lady Up America ecosystem where we can all gather for livestreams, enjoy conversation in our community section (which is like Facebook except it's private just for us), and you can take the 6-Week Challenge to test yourself on what you're learning. Basically, the APP is our girl space where we can grow together!

We invite you to our **Living Room Parties**, which you access inside the APP! Me and my friends come to you LIVE, from my studio, directly to you and your friends gathered in your own living room.

You can chat with us during the livestream party, and we can even pull you and your friends into the livestream, as we're able, based on attendance. We're excited to grow these cottage parties all over the country, meet your friends, and join hands with you across the miles!

You can watch the video version of the **Podcast** inside the APP, on Spotify, and YouTube. You can catch the audio version on all the popular Podcast channels.

Swag is a great conversation starter! I hand-selected neat things for the store, like pop sockets, journals, coffee cups, cute stuffed animals with Lady Up T-shirts, hoodies, and so much more! Most of the items say, *"We've Lost the Luxury of a Meltdown"*.

Help us spread the word! Buy **at ladyupamerica.com/shop**

Our Lady Up America Anthem

I called 2 of my girlfriends, fellow pro songwriters, that I thought would be perfect to write the Lady Up America Anthem with, but one was on tour and the other was in the studio working on a new album. Through a divine series of events, I ended up writing it with 3 great guys: Sweepy Walker, Donald Thomas, and Andy Levine! We wrote it at NSAI and then we had so much fun recording it at Beaird Music Group in Nashville.

Fun fact: I asked the session leader for an R&B vibe, so he called in one of Stevie Wonder's drummers. We sure got that vibe with him!!! The other A-list session players tour and record with Artists you hear on the radio all the time. I sang lead vocals and my co-writers jumped in the vocal booth to deliver those background vocals and Andy's epic ad-libs (above far right)!!! You can find the lyric video on the Lady Up America YouTube channel, or you can download the Mp3 at:

ladyupamerica.com/media.

About The Author

Diane Canada was the 2020 Republican Nominee for the Tennessee State House of Representatives District 56. She is a graduate of the Heritage Foundation's Political Leadership Academy in Washington, D.C., and she is the former Nashville Political Advocate for the National Association of Women Business Owners.

Diane was recently honored with an extraordinary citizen award from the TN State Legislature and the She Leads Tennessee organization for government and community service for her Lady Up America movement, alongside Kathie Lee Gifford, Senator Marsha Blackburn, Riley Gaines, Dr. Alveda King, and other great ladies of service. She has served on the Mayor's Minority and Business Advisory Council, she was a volunteer instructor, teaching entrepreneurship in the TN maximum-security women's prison for 4 years, she currently serves on the Board of the American Bible Project, and on the Board of the Tennessee Immigrant and Minority Business Group. Before politics, she founded a consulting firm, specializing in launching women's businesses and resuscitating businesses in crisis. As a professional songwriter, her music has been used for network TV shows and her own TV show, *Nashville Unleashed*, syndicated in 100 million US households and 3 countries for 2 years. She authored her first book, "Lady Up + Don't Quit" in 2020. She is happily married to Brian, she's a mom and grandmother.

Workshops & Women's Retreats

If you lead a women's group and you would like to book a half-day workshop, a full-day workshop, or a women's retreat with me to train your ladies in my signature techniques, then visit: **ladyupamerica.com/contact** and let's explore the idea.

Made in the USA
Columbia, SC
27 July 2024

38892334R00078